IN SYD'S VOICE

THE EXTRAORDINARY LIFE OF DAVE LAWRENCE

WITH DEAN WILSON

First published by Fairfield Books in May 2025

fairfield books

Fairfield Books
Bedser Stand
Kia Oval
London
SE11 5SS

Typeset in Garamond and Gilroy
Typesetting by Rob Whitehouse

This book is printed on paper certified
by the Forest Stewardship Council

© 2025 Dean Wilson and Dave Lawrence
ISBN 978-1-915237-54-5

A CIP catalogue record for this title is available from the British Library

Printed by CPI Group (UK) Ltd

IN SYD'S VOICE

THE EXTRAORDINARY LIFE OF DAVE LAWRENCE

WITH DEAN WILSON

fairfield books

For Gaynor, Buster and the
MND Association family

Contents

Finding Syd's Voice

There are some moments in life for which you will always be able to say exactly where you were, what you were doing. It might be a World Cup win, the death of a monarch, or the news that you or your partner are pregnant. To those categories I can add Sunday June 30th last year, driving away from Beckenham Cricket Club where West Indies were training ahead of their match with England Lions that began the next day.

I received a call from Dave, who said he had something to tell me. The line went quiet, and then I heard the short breaths and the obvious sound of crying as he uttered the words. 'Dean, I've got Motor Neurone Disease…'

I was stunned. I had to pull over.

The phone was passed to his wife Gaynor, who told me that the doctors had confirmed the news and our beloved Syd was facing a death sentence.

We had been talking for a while about his failure to recover from knee surgery and how he was being tested for a variety of conditions. But I never expected this. I broke down in tears and had to compose myself for the drive home, but the truth is that I sobbed all the way.

Syd and I had already agreed to write a book about his life, long before this diagnosis. It was a great story even without this cruel twist of fate.

We had become friends after I wrote a story about his body-building exploits in 2014. We had a great time in Chelsea Harbour chatting about his muscle-bound life, and we stayed in touch. There was a connection between us, and a mutual respect that any good relationship is built on.

Several years later when he asked if I might be interested in helping to write his autobiography, I was only too happy to say yes.

But we thought we had time. Lots of time.

That all changed in 2024 following his diagnosis when we both understood that time was running out…fast.

Understandably, Syd needed a little time to come to terms with his new reality, but he was certain that he wanted his story to be told. We hatched a plan that would see us talk as often as possible, in

October, November and December 2024 to try and get his version of events before his voice became too weak. Those conversations were revealing, emotional, funny and at times traumatic. I found myself drawing parallels between our lives, both from Caribbean-born parents and Caribbean households, both searching for identity in a country and a sport that sometimes pushed you away.

Most of what he had to say is in the book, but there were conversations that will remain private and were a real glimpse into the core of a man who had had his future ripped away from him but still wanted to give and be supportive of others.

Some days our calls were cancelled due to medical necessity, some days they were cancelled due to the overwhelming outpouring of love and support that meant he had to be somewhere else.

Over time I could hear his voice getting weaker and it became more of a struggle to recognise what he was saying. But we kept on, and by Christmas we had more than enough to make for a captivating book. March was the target for delivery of the manuscript, so January and February were all about writing and fact-checking and writing, and writing.

I had additional conversations with key figures in the book, such as Gaynor, Jack Russell, Derek Pringle, Paul Romaines, Phil Tufnell, Nigel Felton, Roni Size, Alistair Baker, Matt Hudd, Sean Viera, Andy Brassington and George Orchard. Each of them either confirmed or corrected the version of events presented by Syd, and once I re-checked with him, we arrived at the truth. And that is the fundamental point of this book. It is Syd's truth, Syd's story.

When I had finished the first draft, I went to his home in Bristol and read it to him from start to finish. Gaynor and his son Buster were there to hear it too.

I managed to get 300 words in before we were all in tears.

Thankfully we got through it and Syd listened to every word, making the odd interjection using his voice bank. It was another day I will never forget.

Now the book is printed and published and I couldn't be more proud of the work that has gone into it. It has been a privilege.

Dean Wilson
April 2025

CHAPTER ONE

The Diagnosis

I had been awake for a little while already.

The light had been streaming into my room all morning which would have made it difficult to sleep in any case, but that wasn't the reason.

Like it had been so many nights before, my mind was whirring with possibilities and questions about how I had ended up here, in June 2024, in a Bristol hospital waiting and hoping and praying that eventually the doctors would have some good news for me.

It had been four months already in this place, getting tested and retested for a multitude of problems, but each time the results brought me no closer to knowing what was wrong. It was a particular form of torture.

I had arrived in March because I could no longer walk. My legs had stopped responding to the simple instruction to move one in front of the other.

But why? Rewind eight months and to what we thought was the genesis of my issues.

I had been struggling more and more with my left knee, which many will know had been a problem for me for more than 30 years after splitting my kneecap as a fast bowler back in 1992.

I had managed to get to the cusp of 60 years of age without it affecting my way of life. I had definitely made good use of the knee over the years. I had completed half marathons, I had worked out in gyms to a crazy extent, and I had even taken part in Superhuman Games, so the knee had served me well enough.

But now things had become increasingly painful and I was visibly limping on it to try and take the pressure off and reduce that pain. I needed to get things resolved, and a knee replacement was always going to be on the cards at some point. The doctor thought the time was now and I had to agree with him. I was going to have a knee replacement.

That might sound dramatic, but the reality is that it has become one of the most straightforward and successful operations that people can have. And for the vast majority of patients the life that they have with the new knee is so much better and gives them so much more mobility. There had been plenty of wear and tear on the existing knee, and this simple procedure would give me a new lease of life.

The operation was an apparent success and I set about my recovery through the late summer of 2023, keeping an eye on my nightclub Dojo and enjoying my latest role as the president of Gloucestershire County Cricket Club. Their first Black president in more than 150 years of history. Life was good.

I was careful to keep weight off the knee to begin with and then was looking forward to getting back into the gym where I loved spending time and lifting weights. But as each week passed and progress should have been made, the opposite was happening. The knee just wasn't getting any better and I was getting frustrated.

By the autumn, things were actively getting worse. It was more and more painful to stand, even with my ever-present walking stick. It was clear that the leg just wasn't functioning properly.

My doctor thought that something must have happened during the surgery to cause the issue, and perhaps I would need to go under the knife again to fix it. That wasn't great news, but so be it. We looked at getting something booked in for the new year.

By the time it rolled around, not only was I struggling with the left leg, but my right was also causing me discomfort. Now I know they didn't operate on that leg, so what on earth was going on?

Doctors were pretty confident it was nerve damage that was causing the problem. They didn't know how it had happened, but the theory was that it was either the operation itself, or it was a neurological reaction to the surgery that was now the issue, hence the need for more and more tests.

And yet as each scan and blood test was undertaken, the answers became no clearer.

My frustration only grew as I spoke to family and friends about my situation. I had been in hospitals before, but each time I knew why I was there and what needed to be done to make me better. Initially I was very upbeat and optimistic. I had spoken to a few different people about what I was doing there and how long they expected me to be there.

I would have a biopsy, a few tests, they'd tell me what the problem was, then we'd treat it and I'd be on my way home and back on the road to recovery.

I thought it would be alright. I thought they would give me a fairly straightforward diagnosis and even if it might be a long road back, I could handle that. I already knew what it was like to go through the process of rehabilitation for various injuries. And none more so than with my original knee injury, which had meant a lot of lonely hours getting myself fit again.

I had done it before so I knew I could do it again. This time though I didn't even know what was wrong with me. What I did know is that I was getting worse.

For a big and powerful man who had been an international athlete, this was unbearable.

There were tears, of course there were. The uncertainty created an empty space and my mind was filled with all sorts of thoughts, some positive, a lot negative.

The fear of the unknown is one we all have and I was starting to let my imagination run wild at what might be the worst-case scenario.

What sort of life was I going to have if I couldn't walk or run any more?

The physiotherapists and nurses were so encouraging though. They were trying whatever they could to stimulate the nerves and get me moving. They told me stories about incredible recoveries where patients would just suddenly find things working again.

Perhaps it was stress-related, perhaps it was a virus that just needed to work its way through my system. Perhaps, perhaps, perhaps.

All I knew is that my legs were not working as they should be and if I was going to have to spend more time in a wheelchair, and the road back to walking and then running would be a long one, then OK. I could adapt. I could get the work done bit by bit.

This Monday morning, I was sat up in the bed with my wife Gaynor beside me when my consultant Mr Stevens came in to have a chat. He had some news, that much was clear. He was serious, but then he was always serious. He didn't really deal in sugar-coated niceties. He was clinical and precise. He said, 'As you know Dave, we've been testing for a variety of conditions and we've now done the last of these that we need to do to rule every possibility out and I'm sorry but we cannot find the conclusive result we have been looking for. The chances of you walking again are very slim, and there is a very great likelihood that it is Motor Neurone Disease.'

With those three words my heart hit the floor and then it seemed like my body fell with it. I couldn't believe what I had heard. He then said: 'Time will tell, but if it is this disease, then you will progressively get worse and it will bring about the end of life.'

'How sure can you be about this?' I asked, my head spinning. Mr Stevens said: 'I don't know how much you know about Motor Neurone Disease, but there isn't a formal or specific test for it, but by eliminating every other possibility you are left with one remaining explanation.'

Immediately I said that I wanted to get a second opinion. Surely he was wrong. We found a neurological centre in London, in King's Square, and they transferred me there from Bristol. I was seen on the Friday for a nerve conductor study and then the next Monday morning the doctor came to see me.

'Hello Dave, I've got some bad news I'm afraid,' he said. No warning, no preparation, nothing. 'It is as we suspected, it is Motor Neurone Disease.'

For the second time in a week, those three words hit me like a sledgehammer, but this time it was worse. It was the removal of hope. I sank into the bed. All I could think of were images of former Rugby League star Rob Burrow and how he was at the end. A fraction of the size that he used to be. Unable to talk, move or express himself beyond a computer. It was the worst thought.

And can you believe it, they didn't even wait for Gaynor to be there with me. She was staying in London too, in a hotel round the corner.

They didn't realise that she was there to be with me and was nearby, so they came in and told me the news on my own. I then had to phone Gaynor, who was only 10 minutes away, and tell her to come up because it wasn't good news.

It felt like an eternity waiting for her to arrive, but once she did the tears were there for both of us as we went through the news again. Then we had to phone my 26-year-old son Buster and tell him what was happening, which was the hardest thing we've ever had to do as parents.

He got on the train the same day and arrived at the hospital that afternoon. We just cried and held each other. He means everything to me and Gaynor and that afternoon as a family was just horrible.

We had been handed a new reality that none of us wanted, and we had no idea what we were going to do about it. We were numb and in collective shock. I had a week in the hospital in London before I could get moved back to Bristol. It was a week from hell, as I tried to get my head around what was happening.

What did it all mean? How do you cope with what is effectively a death sentence? There is nothing that prepares you for facing this situation until you are there. Why would you talk about death when you are in the business of living?

Certainly that is what I had done for 60 years and I wasn't ready to stop just yet. I had plenty more to see and do and had lots to look forward to, but it was all being ripped away from me.

I had no preparation for this scenario. Of course there had been challenges to face up to before in my life, but they were always battles that I knew I could fight and win.

When you're given a diagnosis for something that has no treatment, and you know that no matter how hard you fight and no matter how hard you stay positive, you can't win – what then?

Normally I'm quite an upbeat person and I have always had that drive and positive outlook to say, I'll get over this injury or I'll get back on the field or back in the gym. There has always been some light at the end of the tunnel. There is no progress to be made here and that takes some getting used to.

So much of my life has been about working hard and putting the hours in to see progress, but you have to realise that this is not about hard work, it is going to beat you. Unless there is a miracle drug that gets discovered in the next few months, it is going to get me. You need a completely different mindset to process this.

And that means taking each day as it comes and trying to live in the moment. I know they are clichés but they really are the only way to approach it. It is a progressive disease that will get me unfortunately. There is no amount of training or hard work that can change that.

Back in June 2024 I was talking normally and my voice was still good. I was still strong in the rest of my body so I was convinced they had it wrong.

I was lying in the bed for hours on end thinking, I'll be alright. It really took a while for me to come to terms with it. I kept hoping that they had the wrong results or the wrong tests, and at any moment the doctor would come through the door and tell me it had been a big mix up and here were my actual results. 'This is what is really wrong with you, and you're going to be fine.'

But each time the door opened, it was a nurse, or doctor or family member whose face told me that there was no mistake. No change in my circumstances. This was my new world and I had to get on with it.

I returned to the hospital in Bristol because my home was in the process of being adapted for me to use, and it wasn't safe for me in the condition I was in.

We'd already had a stairlift put in, but that adaptation would now have to go to a new level. We had to think quickly and sensibly about what the future might look like and, whatever future it was, I wanted it to be in the house that Gaynor and I had built. That was my home.

Back in Bristol, all the optimism with the physios from beforehand just died. They knew that there was not a lot they could do for me any more.

Once they knew my diagnosis, the energy just left everybody, and I get it now. But at the time it was part of my ever deepening, darkening pit of despair.

I didn't want to be there. I just wanted to get home. I would feel better at home, wouldn't I?

CHAPTER TWO

Going Home

It is September 2024 and I've been back in my own home for a couple of months now, but I'm yet to have what you would call a good night's sleep.

I haven't really had one of those for a long time with my mind racing about my situation and the future. It is all so full of stress and sadness.

It was my hope that I would get some time back at home living as close to normally as possible, but the reality is that my body has really deteriorated.

It is now plain to see what I have been going through, even though it took some time for the diagnosis to be confirmed.

My motor functions throughout my body have slowed down to a snail's pace and I am already confined to my motorised wheelchair when I'm out of bed.

I now live downstairs in my house which has been adapted and converted as best we can for my condition.

The chair is incredible and was sourced as soon as possible for me by the Professional Cricketers' Association (PCA) through their charity the Cricketers' Trust. It allows me to move about when I go to places such as to the hospital or my beloved County Ground in Bristol. I can't go anywhere without it.

The bed is automated too and allows me to sit up or lie down at the push of a button. It lies at an angle across our front room, looking towards the window and the natural light. The River Avon is a good throw of a cricket ball away from my front door, but there is a car park between us so the view is not a spectacular as you might think.

I woke up at 4am again today. That has become a bit of a pattern.

I open my eyes and immediately I'm thinking about the situation I am in. I'm thinking about what is coming next for me but also trying not to think too far into the future, as I am unlikely to see as much of it as I thought I would.

I doze off and stir a couple more times before I wake at around 7am.

In the past, if I wanted my day to begin at that time then it would. I could get up and go to the toilet, walk downstairs and make myself and Gaynor a hot drink. I could mix a protein drink for the gym and think about what routine I might do that day. Will it be the biceps? Maybe the lats or the delts. Unless of course it is leg day. Never skip leg day.

How times have changed. Now I wait for another hour or so for my carers to come in and help me.

I now rely on other people to wash me and shower me and help me go to the toilet. And now I skip leg day every day.

It takes a lot of getting used to, that this is my life. That I will need carers for however long I have left.

Gaynor has done a lot of the caring for me too. She has been incredible. Supporting me and loving me and caring for me in a way that she would never have expected to. She has done it without hesitation and with a consistency that has been remarkable.

But she can't do it all, especially as my ability to move grounds ever more to a halt. So I need carers who know what they are doing and who can help me do the most basic of things.

I have found that hard to process and come to terms with.

You are exposed and bare, literally and metaphorically. You are stripped of the things that you used to have control over and in the first week there were lots of tears.

But it is their job and you have to get on with it. They've seen it all before. We talk about lots of different things apart from my condition which has become good fun and a way of taking my mind off the immediate issue.

They are keen to hear about what I'm looking forward to, such as a Massive Attack gig that I'm going to next week and really can't wait for.

Even though I was in hospital for a long period of time and had people doing these sorts of things for me there, that was easier to process because that is what happens in a hospital. But when you're at home in your own space and have people coming in to do these things for you, it is a different scenario and one that we don't really expect to have to cope with until we are much older.

I've been back home for a little while now and even though I thought I wanted to be here more than anywhere else, it is taking more time than I thought it would for me to feel ok about it.

In the hospital I was in a safe space with doctors and nurses there to help 24 hours a day.

Coping with life in your own home when you've gone through such a huge change in circumstances is a real shock to the system and you can't just flick a switch and feel good about it. My brain is still sharp, refusing to follow the same deterioration as my body, and it doesn't want to accept this new life.

I didn't expect to be in the hospital for such a long time, and I didn't expect to receive the diagnosis I did. Truth be told, I didn't expect much of anything that has happened to me in the last 15 months.

It has been just over a year since I first went into hospital for the operation on my knee.

I knew there would be a day when I would need to get it replaced due to the wear and tear it has suffered over my sporting life, but it wasn't supposed to end up like this.

I remember the date. August 19th, 2023. That was the last time that I walked unaided, when I went in for the operation.

From that day, my life has changed and nobody knows for sure why that is. What caused this disease to take hold of me? What set the wheels in motion? I am constantly asking these questions, but they drift away unanswered. There is more and more research being done into MND but the answers will come long after I'm gone.

The doctors told me that it is a slow and progressive disease. But the operation and going under anaesthetic may have acted as a catalyst and sped things up so that the disease has been attacking me as fast as one of my bouncers.

I had wanted to get home as soon as possible after the confirmation of my condition, but I was forced to wait. The house needed some more modifications to enable me to live there safely.

We had a toilet next to the kitchen which we converted into a wet room so that I could wash and shower downstairs, but we had to adjust a few more things such as getting some ramps built round the back of the house for wheelchair access. Out the front there are about 10 steep steps to climb to reach the front door. I was never going to be able to cope with them again, and it was too steep an angle for a ramp.

Thankfully it was possible to put one in round the back and that gave me easier access so I could still get out into the world.

I was genuinely worried that I might not even be able to live in the house any more because I couldn't get in or out, so that was a huge relief.

I love this house so much because it was to be our forever home. We saw it as our final destination, the last place we would move to, where we would spend the rest of our lives together. We would have grandchildren come to stay with us here. And we poured our hearts and souls into it.

We've lived in this house for about seven years, but it took a while for us to get it looking and feeling the way we wanted because originally it was derelict and needed a heck of a lot of work.

It was just a shell really when we bought it and we took our time doing it up, living in each of the rooms while work was going on in the others.

It took about eight months from start to finish, but we were so happy to have it done just how we envisioned.

It is in an area called Hotwells, which I really like. I have been living here for much longer than our ownership of this house. We used to live around the corner and would walk past this site most days and it just intrigued me why it wasn't being lived in. It looked like it had potential to be a great home with a bit of imagination.

I have lived all over Bristol, starting in Montpelier with my sister, but Hotwells is it for me and Gaynor now.

We had originally lived together in Montpelier when I moved into a flat that she had bought. I knew she had a good eye, because even that small flat was very stylishly decorated.

You might think that everything in Montpelier is stylish now because it is a trendy area that has a lot going for it. But back in the 1980s it was far less desirable, sat next door to St. Paul's which was often an area of unrest. In 1987 I moved in and even after we outgrew the flat we continued to stay in the area, buying a house nearby a couple of years later.

We were there for about five years before moving to Redlands, where we had our son Buster. That was his first home.

Once we moved to Hotwells I had a feeling that this might be where we ended up, but it wasn't until we made the decision to buy our current house that I knew we'd found our perfect place. Each time I walked past this house in its run-down state, I would imagine what it might be like to live there.

I thought it could be a terrific family home with a bit of time and love, and money spent on it, but I had to convince Gaynor that it was worth the hassle.

I told her that it would be a project we could do together and we could do it up exactly the way we wanted, but you had to use a bit of artistic licence.

We had a viewing and far from sealing the deal for Gaynor it turned her off it because it was in such bad shape, but I could see past all that. I thought when we were done with it, we would have something truly special.

When it was finished I was so proud of what we had done. It felt like home almost immediately and I was so happy there. That is why I was so keen to get back there from the hospital to start the next phase of my life, no matter how difficult it was going to be. At least I would be somewhere I wanted to be. Or that is what I thought would be the case.

The reality was somewhat different.

While I was in hospital I was living in a bit of a bubble. You don't really see the rest of the world and when anyone comes into your room they are there to try and make you feel as good as possible.

The nurses and the doctors are trying to work out what is wrong and they make themselves busy making you comfortable and looked after.

When your family or friends come to visit they do so out of love and concern and they want you to enjoy that time with them.

But from the moment I left the hospital and began my journey home, reality started to kick in. It was one of the most upsetting journeys of my life.

As I looked out the window as we wound through the streets of Bristol, I started to think, 'This is it Dave. This is your life now. Other people getting on with things while you are left relying on someone to take you wherever you need to be.'

I hadn't been out of a hospital for four months. And even though I had visitors who came to see me and told me about things going on in their lives, it didn't quite resonate.

But in the ambulance I saw people getting on with everyday life, just walking around, driving their cars and living their lives, and it dawned on me that I could never join them again.

And as the vehicle turned into the roads around my house, the roads I knew so well but hadn't been on for months, I started crying. It hit me just how real this was. In my head I was talking to myself. 'This is what it is going to be like for you now, Dave. This is your new reality.'

I was scared. I was afraid of my new circumstances and how I would cope. I told myself, 'You're going to be confined to the power chair. You're going to be living downstairs. You're going to be relying on carers. There will be less and less that you can do for yourself.'

A man's home is his castle they say. A place of refuge and a place of peace and calm. It is where you should feel most comfortable and most relaxed because it is a reflection of you and your tastes. We had the home just how we wanted it and I loved the area.

Maybe I thought that once I saw something so familiar and comforting then I would feel the same way and be happy to be home.

But it wasn't like that at all. I recognised it alright, but the feeling was different to what I expected. I was nervous and anxious about it.

Now that I've had some time to reflect on it, I think it was the feeling of uncertainty that took over on that journey home. I began to think of worst-case scenarios,leading me into some dark places. I was left questioning everything. Why me? Why this disease? I felt so depressed by the life that I was now forced to lead.

My emotions I think were understandable, considering how quickly my life had been turned on its head.

I had plenty of professional support, which was essential, and I am grateful for the way people rallied around me. But no amount of talking could shake me out of my sadness.

I was prescribed some anti-depressants to help me with those emotions. I just couldn't see any other way of dealing with the situation, and the medication did help.

It put an artificial end to the sadness until I started to genuinely come to terms with my situation and could start to see the colour in the world again.

It took time to get to this point and the professional help was part of it. Each time I left the house and returned from trips, my anxiety eased a little. I was starting to get used to the situation, but I also needed the medication to help me through it.

Some would say that time is also a healer, and I would agree that when you have time then of course it can help. But time is not on my side.

Time is deterioration for me. Time is not my friend. I might get settled into a certain routine with my condition remaining stable, but then things will change and I will get a little worse and have to adjust again.

At some point in 2025 I don't know if I will be able to talk. I don't know if I will have any movement in my arms. Time means something very different to me than to most people. Usually people get better with time, but not me.

Each day is a step closer to the inevitable end, but my attitude and approach to that end is changing.

My dreams are now on a repetitive theme, and an understandable one.

Every night I dream about walking. I dream about walking places and seeing people, and getting excited by the use of my legs to take me wherever I want to go.

I haven't had a dream yet where I'm in this wheelchair. I am either walking or running to get somewhere or to meet someone.

Before I lost the use of my legs, I used to dream quite a lot about flying. Not about being a pilot and climbing into the cockpit of a 747, but actually taking off like Superman and flying wherever I wanted to. Imagining that sense of freedom and physical prowess that meant my body could literally do anything, including fly.

Now the dream has changed, and it is all about being able to walk and being able to put one foot in front of the other. Something that I will never do again.

When I wake up I am forced to remind myself that it was only a dream and there will be no walking for me today. Sometimes the dreams are so vivid that I genuinely feel like I have forgotten the predicament I'm in, and then the realisation hits again. It is like being told a fresh diagnosis, over and over again.

CHAPTER THREE

Early Days

I may have been a committed part of the Bristol community for nearly 50 years, but I was actually born in Gloucester in January 1964.

My parents, Joe and Hilda, had made their way to the UK from Jamaica to set up a better life for their family than the one they were likely to have in the Caribbean.

They settled in Gloucester where there was work available and a burgeoning Caribbean community, as there was in lots of cities throughout England.

Jobs needed doing and immigration was a way to get them done, but it was a far from straightforward existence for the pioneers from the Caribbean who initially came over to help rebuild a war-ravaged country.

Being born here, it was a slightly different experience for me than it was for my mum or dad.

We found regular fun and enjoyment at the weekends at a place called 'The Jamaica Club', where a lot of the Caribbean community who had made their way over to the UK in the 50s and had settled in Gloucester would go to meet up and socialise.

Of course church came first though. It would be a case of getting up and getting yourself ready in your smartest clothes before going to Sunday School.

My sisters – Beverley, Diane, Doreen, Pauline – and my brother Steve and I would then rush back home with our parents and get changed into something more comfortable before heading back out for the afternoon to the social club.

It was called the Jamaica Club because there was supposed to be a tie-up between the Jamaican government and the club that would provide some financial support for the ongoing costs, and part of the agreement was that there would be some reference to

Jamaica in the name. That seems a reasonable request – a bit like a sponsor getting the naming rights to a stadium but on a much lower scale.

As I understand it though, that finance never materialised and the name stuck without so much as a Jamaican dollar making it across the Atlantic.

That didn't matter though because the club was home to people from all over the Caribbean. It was started in the 1960s but the actual venue was built in 1970 on a site in Chase Lane and it is still there to this day, although it is now called the All Nations Community Centre after a few difficult periods in which it was very nearly lost completely.

We would go there every Sunday with my dad without fail. He would meet up with his friends, play dominoes, drink Guinness, make noise, while the kids would run around and have fun. There would be Caribbean food and music playing in the background in another room. It was a big part of my life as a youngster in Gloucester.

You were with people who looked like you and who understood you and had similar experiences to you.

There wasn't anyone asking why your nose or lips were so big. It was a refuge from being in the minority in the wider community where too often your difference was something to be feared or concerned about.

The thing that has stayed with me from those days at that club was the ability to be yourself. I can just remember feeling a freedom there that I couldn't enjoy elsewhere. I didn't have to hold my bottom lip in to make it look smaller. Nobody was staring at you like you were a curiosity.

The club provided a safe and friendly environment for people who had left their homeland for the UK at the invitation of the British government to help rebuild the country following the Second World War.

On the face of it, it was a win-win situation with the UK in desperate need of a workforce to get the country back up and running again following the damage from the War, and for many thousands of families arriving from the Caribbean, the UK provided greater opportunities to find work, make money and better their lives, even if it didn't prove to be quite as simple as that.

Even though it was often a traumatic experience for many who made the journey, the roles and the choices were quite straightforward. People like my parents knew who they were and where they were from and they knew why they had travelled to the UK. So even in the face of the many difficulties and barriers put up in front of them, their reasons and the bigger picture remained. They made a choice and they were going to plough on come hell or high water.

* * *

For those of us who were born in the UK and considered it home from the start, things were a little different.

We struggled for identity. Yes, there were other kids like me in my area and in my class at Linden School, but we were a minority. There were many occasions when Black boys in a class were grouped together and treated like outsiders.

We were the first generation born in England and we were told time and again, 'You're not wanted here.'

For people like me we found that incredibly hard to take and our response was, 'Hold on, what do you mean not wanted? We were born here and this is our home.'

That response didn't really cut the mustard with the people who just saw all Black and Brown people as the same, and wanted to get rid of us.

And so as time wore on it became increasingly difficult to feel like you belonged. You were still an outsider to so many people and that takes its toll.

It didn't necessarily come from the people who knew you and who you grew up with, either at school or in the local community, which was pretty multicultural.

It was a much wider issue based around the images and content that we were being fed on TV and in newspapers and magazines which we would consider hugely racist now, but were just the norm back in the 60s and 70s.

Programmes such as *Love Thy Neighbour* and *Rising Damp* portrayed Black people in the most negative of ways with the language used to describe us being quite shameful.

You would hear phrases like 'nig-nog' and 'chocolate drop' and then they would be repeated at school time and time again to refer to the Black kids.

It was of its time and entirely in keeping with the reality of life for so many people in England, but it still felt at odds to me with how people should be treated. It was so disrespectful.

I can remember watching the *Black and White Minstrel Show* as a kid and my dad explaining to me that all the characters were actually white people and that they were blacking up their faces.

Even as a child I knew that this wasn't something that was being done as a positive thing, I knew it was being done to mock and belittle.

I would ask my mum why they were blacking their faces up and she would just say it was entertainment.

Thankfully this racial imbalance was not something I would just go along with throughout my life. Through the influence of a number of different people, I made sure that I would walk tall and hold my head up as much as possible, standing up against those that would try and do me and others down just because of the colour of our skin.

Unfortunately that wasn't always going to be possible and there are moments in later life where I failed to live up to that ideal, but we can only do the best we can.

The first real awakening for me came in the shape of Bob Marley and his powerful, meaningful, and righteous music that cut through so much of the crap that Black people were dealing with.

As a young Black teenager searching for my identity in a world that didn't really like people who look like me, it wasn't easy to find well-known and visible role models, but Bob Marley was certainly one of them.

Suddenly there was a man who was telling anyone who would listen to stand up for your rights and to believe in yourself.

It was just so powerful to kids like me that we all immediately wanted to become Rastafarians and started twisting our hair up, searching for red, gold and green clothes to wear because it was a form of identity and you could belong to a community that saw the world the same way you did.

I was only about 10 or 11 when I started to really get into Bob Marley and his music, so it was a fairly simplistic view, but as I look back on that time now, I wouldn't change a thing and I still totally agree with the sentiments that I fell in love with at the time.

Bob had a way of connecting with those of us in England who were constantly told that Jamaica or the Caribbean was 'home' but had never been there.

We found ourselves slipping into the cracks between a 'home' that we didn't know and a 'home' that was hostile. We were looking for guidance and for inspiration and Bob provided it with catchy melodies, driving rhythms and lyrics that spoke to us about empowerment and respect, and love and harmony. It is easy to see why we all wanted to be like Bob.

While I was growing up in Gloucester, I didn't realise that Bob's first gig in the UK was actually not far down the road in St Pauls in Bristol, near where I would live when I was a bit older.

It was at a similarly West Indian venue, called the Bamboo Club, where he played in 1972 during a tour on which he was supporting Johnny Nash, and he stole the show. He returned again in 1973 during his 'Catch a Fire' tour, but the club burned down in 1977 and with it went a huge amount of history.

I would often hear stories about the Bamboo Club and the legendary reggae acts who had performed there in the 60s and 70s. It was the social hub for the Caribbean community in Bristol for a decade and a place I know I would have spent plenty of time in too had it still been there when I eventually lived in St Pauls. Sadly I never got the chance to see Bob Marley play live as he was taken at the tender age of just 36 in 1981, but the impact he had on me at a formative age was quite significant.

I watched a programme about Bob's time in the UK during the 1970s, and it is clear he had a great affection for the country and the people.

One of the contributors, musician and DJ Don Letts, spent time with Bob and put it best when he said: 'We were the children of the Windrush generation and along comes Marley with these tunes that somehow resonated with our situation growing up in the UK... He gave us the beginnings of an identity.' That is exactly how I felt too.

My father had followed his brother over here and it was a similar story for my mum, who followed a friend of hers to Gloucester. The city was a real melting pot of multiculturalism and growing up my friends came from lots of different backgrounds, but most of them were either white or mixed race.

Maybe I'm looking back with rose-tinted glasses, but instinctively I feel as though Gloucester dealt with the integration of different ethnicities and cultures as well as any place.

That's probably because I lived there and have an affinity with it, but it didn't have the explosive race riots that were associated with St Pauls, or Brixton or Handsworth in the 1980s.

As a young teenager I loved reggae, but as I got older I became a massive Northern Soul fan. It was a really big thing in Gloucester and Bristol during the 70s, but if you wanted to really experience the scene you had to get yourself up to the Wigan Casino, which is what I did as a 15- and 16-year-old who was music mad.

It was a bit of a journey from Gloucester to Wigan, but me and my friends Neil Williams and Gary Davis would think nothing of getting the train there and back, or hitching a ride. If we set off at 5pm then we would get there at midnight just as things were coming alive. We'd get there alright.

You'd have your little bag of clothes to get changed into and off you went to dance the night away.

The music was everything. Thumping soul tunes from across the pond in the USA that you often couldn't hear anywhere else, not even on the radio.

The DJs were very protective of their tunes and if they managed to get hold of a floor filler that no-one else had then they would be the king of the decks until the next mega tune came over.

It was all about the B-sides of the records, which would often become more popular than the A-sides. You would also see some great live performers too. I remember seeing Edwin Starr up on stage during one party.

The crowd at these events were pretty good by and large and I can remember having some great nights and making instant friends on the dancefloor.

I loved to dance. The feeling of moving to the rhythm of the music and the freedom that came with being able to express yourself in your own little space was glorious and it never left me.

There are lots of things that this disease has robbed me of but the inability to dance to the music that I love is one of the worst.

When my friend and dancing-partner-in-crime George Orchard comes round to visit me, sometimes he plays the tunes that we used to groove to back in our teenage years and it transports me back to a time when my nights were filled with dance and laughter. I miss those days, of course I do, but the fact I can't even try to get down and bounce back up again is so frustrating. I can't even join in with my granddaughter's joy at moving to music. Hopefully she will have been passed down the same grooving genes that I have.

The music was absolutely brilliant and almost exclusively Black soul artists from America. But the crowd who were dancing to it was almost exclusively white. I was one of very few Black men or women. Even though it was mainly Black artists, if you liked Northern Soul as a Black man you were branded a 'coconut' – meaning Black on the outside and white on the inside. It is a cutting insult to be hit with, essentially saying you have turned your back on your own and are trying to be white.

This is something that I have had to deal with throughout my life and it is a term I hate because it is just as spiteful as the words used by others to describe Black people.

It absolutely stands as a divisive term between races and it's something that just wound me up. I am well aware of the colour of my skin and I am well aware of the history of racism across the UK and around the world, but we all bleed the same and if I get on with you or vice versa it will have nothing to do with the colour of your skin.

Looking back on that time now, I do wonder how much that search and yearning for identity played on my mind.

The truth is I just didn't really know where I belonged.

I was just four when Enoch Powell delivered his 'Rivers of Blood' speech about immigration into the UK and how people in his Wolverhampton constituency were fearful of the changing faces of their community.

The impact of that speech and similar rhetoric that followed was felt throughout the 1970s and 80s as racial tensions continued to escalate between groups who were either driven by fear or anger at a lack of equality.

There were lots of arguments for repatriation and re-emigration of people like my mum and dad who had come to the UK as British citizens, members of Empire and the Commonwealth, but who were now seen as overstaying their welcome.

Never mind the fact that they had played their part in getting the country back on its feet in the aftermath of the War. As the economy and the jobs market became bumpier, it was easy to blame the problems on the immigrant population who had put down roots and were settled.

This was the narrative that we were being bombarded with throughout the 1970s and while you just had to get on with things and find your way, it made life a little more stressful than it needed to be.

CHAPTER FOUR

Introduction to Cricket

If music was one of my great passions growing up then cricket was the other. But it wasn't something that I was obsessed with until the age of 12, when everything changed for me. In 1976 my world view shifted.

I've talked a little bit already about what life was like for a young Black boy growing up in the UK in the 60s and 70s.

Not only did I have overt racism directed at me by people at school or in the street, but the systematic negativity was a shadow that hung over people like me and was simply a part of everyday life.

It was a real challenge to find positive Black figures and role models in the images of everyday life. Your parents and their friends were your role models of course, as it should be, but we all like to have people to look up to and admire. That's why I fell so hard for Bob Marley.

In the mid 70s I didn't see many positive Black role models on TV. There was Clyde Best the footballer for West Ham, and then others such as Viv Anderson and Cyrille Regis started to emerge.

In the scorching hot summer of 1976, the West Indies were in the UK and taking the cricket world by storm.

But I couldn't have been less interested. I wasn't a cricketer. I knew a little bit about it because it would sometimes be on the news and my dad would mention it every now and then, but it just wasn't on my radar. My school didn't play it and honestly I thought it was just a boring game.

I also didn't really know about the West Indies team. This was very much the analogue age, so it was easy for things to pass you by.

My father was a boxing fan first and foremost and he would take me and my brother Steve down to the local boxing gym with designs on us becoming the heavyweight champions of the world.

I can't say that this was ever a realistic option for me. I could throw a punch, which would come in handy when I was older, but I probably spent a little bit too much time getting to know the canvas to be any great shakes as a boxer.

I can't say that I enjoyed getting hit, but we had no choice as it was a part of our Saturday club.

We were marched down to a place called the India House which was an old pub on Barton Street. It had a gym upstairs where the Gloucester Boxing Club was based and it was run by a man called Mr Richmond. We were told that he was a former Mayor of Gloucester, but I'm not too sure about that.

Anyway, it was quite a thriving club back in the day and loads of local kids would go down there and train in the gym every Saturday. You'd warm up, get the gloves on and then get hit!

It was generally a good experience as it taught you discipline at an early age. Working the bags, doing your training, your sit-ups, your press-ups. It was my first experience of proper sport and being in the club, you were all going through something together. Even though boxing is a solitary exercise in the ring, it was actually a team environment and I loved that.

You were judged on merit and you were respected for the skill that you had. And it felt good to be a part of something on a regular basis. We would have boxing matches between us and I must admit that part I didn't enjoy too much. I didn't like getting whacked, but I loved the training.

I also enjoyed playing rugby in the winter. I played on the wing for a club called the All Blues in Gloucester, which is the same side that former England flanker Mike Teague played for.

After doing that for a few years, 1976 came along and my head turned unexpectedly.

One day my dad just said to me, 'Son, we're going down to The Oval.'

I looked at him a little puzzled and simply asked, 'What is The Oval?'

'It is a cricket ground,' he replied. 'And we're going to watch some cricket with some of my friends.' 'Who's playing?' I asked, as if it made any difference. I didn't know anything about it and he could have told me Disney were playing Marvel and I'd have thought that was normal.

'It's England playing against the West Indies.'

'Oh right, so a team from Jamaica then?' 'Not quite son, it's a team made up of some guys from Jamaica but also from the other islands like Barbados and Trinidad and so on.'

I sort of shrugged my shoulders and that was that, I was going to watch a sport that I had never seen before and arguably the greatest cricketers ever to play that sport in the history of the game. But I wasn't a 12-year-old full of excitement and desperate to get up close to these legends. I didn't even know who they were. I was just tagging along with my dad and going to experience something new.

We got to the ground in good time and the first thing that struck me was just how busy and noisy it all was. There were so many people and so many Black people too. I thought that I came from quite a multicultural place in Gloucester but South London was on a different scale. It was busy and vibrant and colourful.

As we weaved through the crowds, my dad met up with his friends and found the spot they were going to be watching from in the stands, while I and a couple of other kids with the group were sent down to the boundary edge where we could sit on the grass and watch from an even closer viewpoint.

As I sat there waiting for the action to start, I noticed this group of men walk out onto the field, and they were huge. I hadn't seen anything quite like it before and I just looked at them in astonishment.

In my mind they were so big they were literally blocking out the sun. I was just in awe of their presence, their swagger and confidence. I hadn't ever seen a group of Black men move with such authority.

The West Indies supporting crowd were cheering them on with great enthusiasm but I also noticed that the English fans were very respectful of them too, with lots of applause.

As everyone settled into their positions, one of the West Indies players walked towards me and I thought he was going to come and field near where I was watching from, but he turned around and started to run away from me. It was Michael Holding.

I was mesmerised by him. The elegance, the athleticism, the style and the power all rolled into one brilliant bowler, I just couldn't take my eyes off him.

He absolutely destroyed England in that match. He picked up eight wickets in the first innings and then another six in the second to back up an incredible 291 scored by Viv Richards in the Windies' first innings. These were the masters of the game and they had given England a taste of what the next 20 years would look like.

Of course I had no idea that I would get the chance to become a part of that history on the very same ground, but it was there on that sunny August day that I became hooked on cricket and decided I wanted to be a fast bowler. I wanted to be Michael Holding.

The trip back to Gloucester from London must have been a painful one for my dad who had to field question after question from his rather excited 12-year-old son. The issue now was, how would I feed this new passion of mine? I hadn't played the game before and my school, which was just a normal state school, didn't play formal cricket.

The only cricket we had at school was playground cricket with a painted set of stumps on the wall and we would use a tennis ball that you would wet with water so it would skid on a lot quicker, and that is where I started bowling.

I just tried to mimic the West Indian bowlers, and to my great joy it turned out I was quite good at doing that, although in my own style.

It was great fun playing at break time, but I longed for more, and I wanted to play the sort of cricket that I had seen West Indies play.

If I was going to play the game I had to find a club to give it a go and luckily up the road from where we lived was a small cricket club called Gloucester City.

* * *

One week I walked up to the ground on my own to see if I could play. I was a bit nervous about walking in there and even now I can remember the atmosphere being quite a frosty one. I think they thought I was lost, or was up to no good. In any case, I finally plucked up the courage to ask someone whether I could play. They told me to clear off and come back on Friday when the junior cricket sessions were on, and that was that.

Maybe I was reading too much into it, but I definitely got the impression that they would rather I cleared off and didn't come back. I'd like to think that if a young person turns up at a cricket club out of the blue these days, then there is a warmer welcome for them and they will get shown the way forward.

I guess it is the luck of the draw who you bump into at any given time. One thing for certain is that no professional sportsperson ever gets to the top of their chosen sport without plenty of help and guidance from others along the way.

And in my case I had a few people who really helped me when I needed it.

I was actually in two minds about going back there on the Friday, but the day came around and as I was outside the house pondering my next move, two of my school friends were walking past, Martin Lewis and Alan Butler.

Martin is a friend of mine to this day, and I asked them, 'Where are you guys off to?'

They said they were going to Gloucester City for cricket training.

Well that made up my mind. 'Do you mind if I come along with you?' I asked, and off we went. On this particular Friday evening the session was being run by a guy called Brian Worrall, and he would be a great help to me in those early days.

He gave me a ball and asked, 'So what do you do?' To which I replied, 'I bowl fast.'

In my mind I was thinking about Michael Holding, so that is who I tried to emulate and I just ran in to bowl and did my best 'Whispering Death' impression.

Mikey was given that brilliant nickname because he ran in to bowl so elegantly that he hardly made a sound as he glided towards the crease. And then in the blink of an eye the batter would face a ball that would often signal the termination his innings. In some cases the ball was so ferocious that it might just kill him if he didn't get out of the way in time.

So 'Whispering Death' was the perfect character for Mikey, but for me something like 'Pounding Tumbler' might have been more suitable. As I charged in and let the ball go, I completely lost my footing and fell on the ground with my backside taking the brunt.

I got back to my feet, and walked back to Brian, expecting him to say, 'Thanks but no thanks, cricket clearly isn't the game for you', but instead he said, 'That is the quickest delivery I've ever seen bowled by a teenager. That was the same pace as you see in men's cricket.'

I couldn't believe it, but I was chuffed to hear it.

Obviously concerned about me wearing plimsoles to bowl in, he told me to come back the following week and asked if I had or could get some cricket boots.

I said I couldn't get cricket boots by the next week, my dad's got five other children to look after so there was no chance.

When I returned the next week, Brian gave me my first pair of cricket shoes and really encouraged and coached me from there.

He taught me the fundamentals of bowling and about using my pace and he got me playing in my first games for the club in the junior teams. But while Brian was supportive and encouraging, there were others there who saw me in a very different way and simply didn't like me being a part of the club.

There were no other young Black boys at the club so I stuck out a bit, but I didn't mind that as I was used to having lots of white friends from school. But while other players in the junior sides were starting to play in the senior teams at the weekends I wasn't being selected, even though I was developing pretty well as a cricketer.

I would get the odd game here and there but it took a long time before I was playing consistently at the weekend.

Even when I had proven my quality in the second team, I just couldn't break into the first team when I was certainly good enough. Brian kept pushing my case, he was just a terrific person who took everyone as he found them, but I still couldn't get a fair crack. It was always a struggle.

You don't want to believe there is any other reason apart from skill and ability as to why you are not given a chance, and for a long time I carried on thinking that the other players were simply better than me. But once I moved clubs and started playing for Bristol West Indians and other representative teams it began to dawn on me why I didn't get a chance.

Thankfully Brian was happy to do what he could to further my cricketing education and he put me in touch with a couple of different associations when he heard that there were trials that I might be able to go along to.

I was lucky enough to be put forward for a trial for Gloucestershire Schools Under-14s because Brian thought I was ready to take another step forward. He told me to turn up and give it my best and see how I went. I had to get permission from my school to get the afternoon off to go along to a private school and show what I could do.

Even though I'd been playing for a couple of years at Gloucester City I wasn't exactly laden with kit and so I didn't have a proper cricket bag. I just used to carry my stuff in a Tesco bag.

So I turned up for this trial and had the immediate feeling that I didn't belong as the kids got out of their fancy cars with mum and dad and their sparkling new kit, and lots of it, while I swung my bag over my shoulder and carried a bat that must have been older than everyone on the ground.

I laugh about it now because it shouldn't really matter but at the time I remember looking at the gloves of the other boys and they were the nicely padded sausage-finger type gloves while I had the old style rubber pimple gloves which offered about as much protection as a rolled-up newspaper.

I was a fish out of water. I was totally out of place and I knew it, not to mention the fact that I was the only Black face there.

No-one talked to me or even acknowledged me apart from the person organising the trial who had my name down on a list.

Soon enough everyone started to get themselves ready to play and in amongst the excited chatter of children who already felt so comfortable and at ease, I just felt completely apart and alone, and unsure if I should be there.

I was told to stand down at fine-leg, which is where bowlers normally field between overs, but when the over was completed they didn't ask me to bowl the next one, they just told me to field at mid-on, which wasn't much fun.

The ball came to me occasionally and I fielded as best as I could before heading back down to fine-leg. I did this for what felt like hours, waiting and hoping that they would ask me to bowl.

Eventually when it seemed like they had no choice, they asked me to bowl and this is when things changed.

I ran in and bowled my heart out and caused all sorts of problems for every batter as they simply weren't used to facing real pace. Or at least real pace for that age group.

It was a feeling I rather enjoyed and one that never left me throughout my entire career. Nobody likes facing real pace. Uncomfortable pace. Pace that makes batters do things that they don't mean to do.

I blew them away, picking up wickets regularly and totally changing people's opinion of me. It is amazing what a bit of athletic talent and skill can do.

And after that first trial they didn't dare not put me through to the next stage. Two further trials later and I was selected to play for Gloucestershire Schools.

It was a brilliant moment when they told me I had got in, not only because I felt pride at the achievement for myself but because I was the first person from my school to be picked for the county so the school were very proud of me.

Things continued to go well on the field and I kept taking wickets at every level that I played, and so a year later I got chosen to represent the South West of England. This was a team selected from players from Gloucestershire, Somerset, Devon and Cornwall, so another level up.

Once you're in this side then you are in a position to compete to be in the full England age-group side, and that is what I wanted more than anything.

I was so proud to be representing Gloucestershire and then the South West of England, but I was desperate to become a young England player.

My chance came when I travelled to take part in a tournament where all the different regions would be competing against each other. And at the end of that tournament they would be selecting the England Under-15 squad. It is what became the Bunbury Festival in the years that followed, but back then it was just the England Schools Tournament, and I can remember travelling up on the train with Rob Bailey, who would go on to play for England and become a very successful international umpire.

As an aside, I bumped into Rob at a Gloucestershire game at Bristol a few days after the team had won the 2024 T20 Blast. As the players were coming off the field for lunch a few of them stopped to say hello and then I felt this big hand thrust into mine, and it was Rob. We shared a nice little moment as he reminded me that our relationship went back some 45 years and he wished me all the best. He was good company on the train to this tournament where a lot of young cricketers find out where they stand in relation to the rest of their age group in the country. These are the players you are hopefully going to be competing with for county contracts and England honours in the future so it is good to know what level you are at in comparison.

And of course there is still that element of the haves and the have-nots when it comes to these sorts of events.

I can remember lots of people flocking around Michael Parkinson, who was there with his son Michael junior. And there was Colin Cowdrey with his younger son Graham, who would go on to have a long career with Kent.

I did pretty well, bowled nicely, took some wickets and had a few lads hopping about a bit and backing away to leg. Overall I thought I was easily good enough to be put into the England age-group team, but there was little encouragement from the people running the tournament and I just got the feeling that they didn't really want me. They would talk animatedly with other players when they took wickets, but left me well alone when I did the same.

At the end of the tournament when the squad was selected, I didn't make the cut, and I had to accept that maybe I just wasn't quite good enough.

But after the decision was made, I spoke to the selector who told me the reason I didn't get in. "You bowled well and came very close to selection, but we just feel that the wickets won't suit your kind of bowling." I was a bit surprised to hear that as I thought I did pretty well on whatever wickets I played on, but this was the decision and I just had to take it and move on.

It didn't diminish my love for the game or desire to play more, but I thought I would just have to be even better the next time I got a chance to try and compete for a place at the next level.

Eventually I would make it into the England Youth side and play two games against India in the same 1981 summer that I made my first-class debut for Gloucestershire.

Despite my obvious ability and progression elsewhere in the game, I never did get picked to play in the first team for Gloucester City and I think that had more to do with the colour of my skin than my ability to bowl a cricket ball.

And yet, years later, after being picked to play for England, I was invited to a dinner back at Gloucester City and I made a presentation.

I had my England blazer framed, I gave it to the club and it still hangs on the wall in the clubhouse to serve as inspiration.

I spoke about my experiences there and said: 'I don't want this to be a barrier to any young cricketer playing at the club. I want the next young player to look up and see that blazer and hopefully that will inspire them to achieve their dream.'

Things have completely changed there over the years and anybody and everybody is welcome to play, but when I started, things were very different.

CHAPTER FIVE

Viv the Mentor

No matter who you are or what you end up doing with your life, having the right people around you at the right time is worth its weight in gold.

There are those you expect to have your back. Your parents, your siblings and your friends. People who know you and trust you and will do whatever they can to help you.

But as I have discovered throughout my life, there are times when someone you don't expect can have a significant positive impact on you, and it arrives right when you need it most.

By the time I was 15 or 16, cricket had a hold on me in a way that nothing else did. All my energy was being put into the game, and I guess one or two people had started to notice that I had some real potential.

But even though I loved playing the game and was pretty good at it, I had no idea that it was something I could do for a job. I had no designs on becoming a professional cricketer and didn't really treat it like it was something to work hard at.

And bearing in mind what I had experienced at previous representative trials, I never thought that elite cricket was for me. I certainly wouldn't fit in.

Even so, I enjoyed playing and had some success at club level and for my junior Gloucestershire sides.

As a result, one of those who had started to follow my progress was Graham Wiltshire, who was Gloucestershire coach during the 70s and 80s.

He had played for the club in the 60s as a medium-fast bowler and after captaining the second XI he moved into coaching and was a big figure at the club.

One day in the summer of 1980 after playing for the Gloucestershire academy, he came over to have a chat with me along with Brian

Worrall, my coach at Gloucester City and said that the club wanted to sign me to the staff after my exams.

I paused. Not because I was thinking about the offer but because I didn't really know what that meant.

I didn't know what joining the staff would entail, what job I would have to do, because surely it wasn't just about me playing cricket for a living?

'I'm sorry Graham, I don't know. What would it all mean?' I said.

He explained: 'Well David, it would mean you coming down and spending a fair bit of time at the County Ground in Bristol and basing yourself here for the whole summer. You'll play in the second team and you'll learn about the game and a few more things around the ground, maybe helping out with a few jobs. The best part is that you will get to play cricket almost every day, either matches or training… how does that sound?'

I must admit, that sounded pretty good to me. He told me that he thought I could make a career out of playing cricket, which I hadn't really thought of before then.

I'd wanted to play for Gloucestershire and to play for England, but I didn't really consider what that actually meant and how it all worked. The dream that you are chasing often doesn't really have finer details to it, and I hadn't really thought about what a 'career' as a cricketer might look like.

Now it was becoming a real prospect, and the decision was made almost immediately. I was going to be a cricketer and I couldn't wait to get started.

The problem was I was living with my mum and dad in Gloucester and I didn't exactly have the means to come and go as I pleased with most home matches being played in Bristol.

So imagine my delight when Graham told me that as part of the deal I would actually get paid… not much of course, but it was a lot more than I was getting at the time.

Naturally I jumped at the chance. I mean, who wouldn't want to get paid to do the thing they love the most?

What happened next I'm not particularly proud of, but it is what I did and I have lived with the consequences of my actions since.

I was 16 years old and in the middle of sitting my O-Levels at the end of my time at school. I went in for one of my last exams and as

I sat down to do the paper, all I could think about was my future as a cricketer. I was so excited.

I think it was an English exam, I can't quite remember now, but I sat there for a few minutes and kept seeing myself in a Gloucestershire shirt running in to bowl and knocking the stumps out of the ground. My mind was definitely not on the task at hand.

A thought then suddenly entered my head. If I'm going to play cricket for a living, then what am I doing here in this exam? This is not going to help take wickets on a flat pitch in Bristol. Why am I putting myself through all this stress when I've got a contract with Gloucestershire? And with that thought I got up out of my seat, put my pen down and walked out.

The teacher asked me where I was going, and I said simply, 'I'm off!' And I walked out of the hall and I never went back.

* * *

The change from recreational cricketer to professional player would mean me having to move closer to Bristol, and after speaking with my sister Bev, who lived in Montpelier, I was able to move in with her and begin my professional cricket career.

We lived right next door to St Pauls, which at that time was a tense place to live. A few months earlier it had seen a full-scale riot after youths clashed with the police at the Black and White Cafe. There were to be more flashpoints over the course of the next decade in and around the area, but there was a sense of community there too. People did get on with each other and I found it easy to make friends, just as I had in Gloucester.

I didn't exactly have a grand plan for my life at this stage, but the thought of being able to use my body and my skills to earn a living really interested me. I was keen as mustard for the opportunity I had been given, so on my first day at the club I was determined to be early. I walked up the hill to the ground from my sister's house, and this was the way I always went to the ground while I lived with her. I had the room in her basement and there were no windows so I was just glad to be out and in the fresh air.

I got to the ground nice and early and got changed into my cricket kit ready to get to work as the other guys from the second team arrived such as future England opener Chris Broad. We started by doing some fielding with Graham hitting the balls out for us to gather and return over the stumps.

He hit one out towards a group of us and shouted 'David!' At which point three players descended on the ball and tried to field it.

'Stop! Stop! Stop!' Came the call from the coach, who was walking towards us all. 'This won't do,' said Graham, there's too many David's in this squad. You all need nicknames.'

At which point Broady chirped up and said: 'What about 'Syd'?! You should be called 'Syd' after the big bandleader Syd Lawrence.' I didn't really have any objection, so I just accepted it. And if I hadn't liked it and made a fuss, it would have stuck even faster. After a bit of thought, I reckoned it wasn't a bad name at all and it has been a good name for me, so thank you Broady! There are now plenty of people who don't even know my real name is David.

David Partridge was given the name Bez, I can't quite remember why, and the last David was called Simmo, thanks to his surname Simpkins.

With everyone now suitably named, we could get on with our training session, and from that moment on I was Syd.

I might have had a new name, but I didn't know what it truly meant to be a professional at anything. I didn't quite grasp the idea that professionalism wasn't just about turning up on a gameday and trying your best and hoping that things worked out.

There is so much more to it, but like anything you learn from experience and in the early days of my career I had a couple of moments to learn from that made a huge difference.

The first of these came when I found myself playing in the second team the following summer in 1981 and was grateful to have Tony Brown involved at the club.

Tony was a Gloucestershire legend. He played and captained the club for years and years before moving into administration and eventually becoming chairman. He sadly passed away in 2020, but he had a profound impact on my career and I owe him an incredible amount, because he turned out to be one of those right people at the right time.

Tony really was one of my greatest supporters and I owe so much to him. And it all started at the beginning of the 1981 pre-season training camp.

I was 17 and fairly wet behind the ears, and he said to all of us, young and old, 'Listen guys, you are part of this club and part of this family now and I will back you all. You can phone me at any time, night or day, and if you're in any bother or need any help just pick up the phone and call me. I'd rather hear from you than from someone else about you.'

And so it came to pass later that summer when I was playing in a three-day game and on the Saturday night, instead of getting myself back to bed and ready for the next day's play, I went out and got myself into a bit of bother.

I had gone out with a few friends and was having a good time of things, as any young lad would do, but as the night wore on, things got a little heated with a few other people and there had been a bit of a ruckus in the pub we were in. It wasn't particularly serious, but I got involved in a fight and got myself arrested and locked in the cells. It was a lot of something over nothing, but I was still behind bars.

Knowing I was supposed to be playing cricket the next day I got my phone call and rang Tony.

'Hi Tony. It's Syd here. Do you remember at the start of the season you said that we should call you at any time if we find ourselves in any trouble?'

The line was quiet for what seemed like an eternity, but thankfully Tony responded.

'Yes Syd, I remember. What's happened?'

'I'm in a bit of strife here. I'm in the police station and think I need a solicitor to help me out.'

Tony was as good as his word and got me a solicitor to come and get me out. Unfortunately it was on a Sunday, and in those days very few people worked on a Sunday and if you were locked up on a Saturday night it wasn't until the Monday that you could get out, and so I had to sit in the police station all day when I should have been playing cricket and trying to help my team win a game.

It was an unfortunate incident and one that didn't go any further, but it didn't exactly paint me in the best light. There were already one or two figures at the club who weren't exactly keen on me in the first place, so this was one for them to put in their holster. It wasn't the first time that Tony had to sort something like this for a player so he was used to the situation, but quite rightly he made it clear that this was a situation for me to learn from and not to repeat.

He gave me a deserved dressing down and I felt pretty embarrassed that I had got into that position. I apologised to Tony and said that it wouldn't happen again, but there was still a lot of maturing to be done.

I quickly put this episode behind me and got back to my cricket for the rest of the 1981 season, but the following year, things once again took a bad turn and I found myself in need of Tony's support in more ways than one.

I had been doing a bit of shopping one afternoon in town, checking out some clothes and some music that I had my eye on, but I actually ended up buying very little. My cashflow still didn't allow me to buy whatever I wanted but I enjoyed looking, who doesn't?

As I was walking through town I bumped into a few guys who I knew from the St Pauls area who were out and about. We had a bit of a chat and they asked if I wanted a lift back home. 'Why not,' I thought. Saves me waiting for a bus and this would take me right to my front door.

I jumped in and off we went.

We had been driving for a few minutes when suddenly the driver put his foot to the floor with sirens blaring behind us.

'What on earth are you doing?!' I yelled. 'Just pull over and see what the police want.' 'Can't do that Dave,' came the reply. 'It's not my car.'

I had no idea what I had got myself into, totally unwittingly. The police were chasing us, and there was absolutely no way that the car was going to stop. We careered through the streets, narrowly avoiding traffic and pedestrians, and I'll be honest I was scared. I had every right to be too because we went flying round a corner and clipped the kerb, causing us to tip over and crash in a heap.

It was a horrible experience and one that could have been even worse. I wasn't wearing a seat belt and if the car had spun in another direction or I had moved another way, then I might not even have made it. As it was, I ended up lying on the ground with the whole right side of my body in absolute agony awaiting an ambulance to take me to hospital. The next thing I knew I woke up in hospital with my hands cuffed to the bed and the police wanting to question me about the stolen car.

Once again I called Tony and told him what had happened and where I was, although it felt pretty pointless because he would have no choice but to wash his hands of me.

At least that is what I thought would happen. I knew there were some at the club who had wanted me gone after the first incident, but Tony had my back and talked them down. Not even the smoothest of talkers could do the same this time – even though I was completely blameless.

Thankfully I got the chance to explain to Tony when he came to the hospital to see me and he assured me that he believed what I was saying, but he was clearly upset with what had happened. Once he knew that I was ok physically, he was pretty angry with me, for putting myself in that position.

And naturally he had a few more people at the club who were done with me and wanted to sack me. Even though I was an innocent party in what had happened, it wasn't good for the club to have one of their players involved in a police car chase through the streets of Bristol before ending up in a nasty accident.

I sometimes wonder how different things might have been if I had suffered more than severe bruising and soreness. Or heaven forbid if someone else had been hurt or worse still. It was a stupid situation to find myself in and quite rightly it made me think a little more carefully about who I travelled with in the future.

I was due to be discharged the following day, and Tony came to see me to make sure everything was ok. Before he left, he told me to meet him at the ground at Nevil Road at 9am on Monday morning.

Well that's that, I thought. I'm going to get the sack and my cricket career is going to be over before it has really begun.

And as angry as I was with the guys who had stolen the car and put me in hospital, I was even more upset with myself for being in that situation in the first place.

I turned up nice and early to the ground and waited for Tony to show up by the gates, and right on the stroke of nine, he pulled into the car park and opened the passenger door.

He scowled and without saying anything he nodded for me to get in. I climbed in and shut the door. He pulled out of the gates and remained silent as we hit the road.

Family matters: parents Hilda and Joe made their way to the UK from Jamaica; with my siblings; and my older sister Bev, with Ronald.

Family life: spending time with Buster, partying with Gaynor,
and teaching the young man a thing or two!

My twin rocks, Buster and Gaynor.

I loved giving back to the game and encouraging kids; and receiving the
Cricket Writers' Club Young Player of the Year award from Princess Diana.

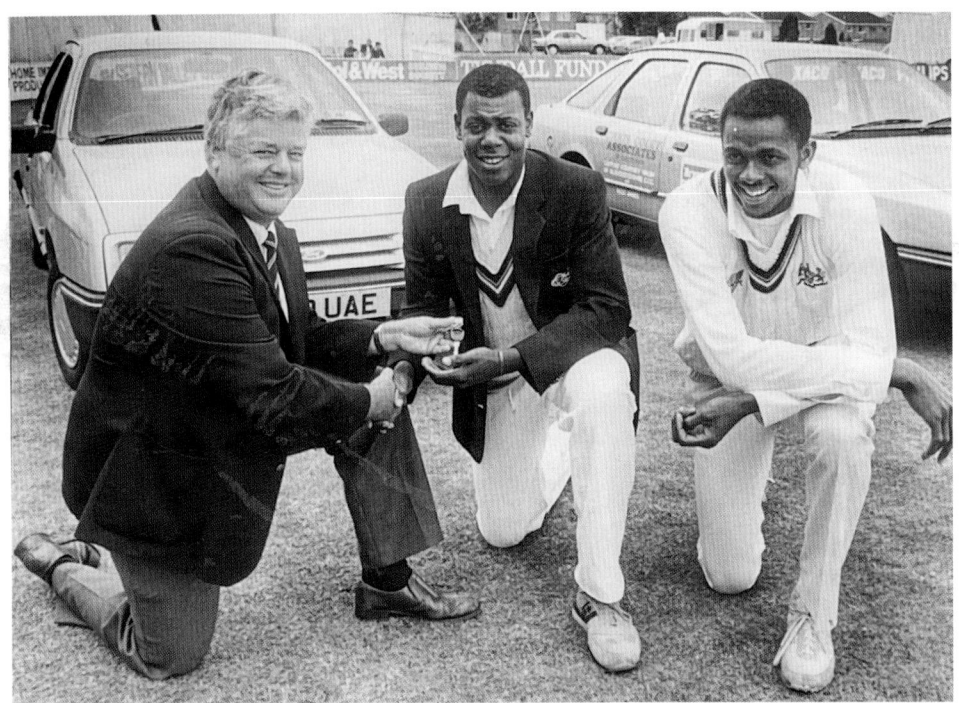

Friends for life: Courtney Walsh and Jack Russell.

Batting was not my strongest suit!; with friend and teammate Mark Alleyne.

Cricket was not my only sport! I loved football, boxing and, of course, bodybuilding.

In full flight.

I had no idea where we were going, but instinctively I knew not to ask any questions. Tony had a stern look on his face, he was a big bloke too, and I thought I'd better not run the risk of doing anything that might annoy him more than he was already. We made it onto the motorway and throughout there was a tense silence that I daren't puncture.

Eventually after driving for a little while Tony pulled the car into what looked like another cricket ground and parked up. We got out and I followed him into this large room that looked out over the ground.

'Sit there and don't move!' barked Tony. The first words he had uttered to me since telling me to meet him that morning when we were in the hospital. I must have sat on my own for about 10 minutes until I saw two figures off in the distance walking towards me. I could see that one of them was Tony, but the other I couldn't quite make out until he got much closer.

As he did my first thought was, 'That's a swagger and a half,' and when I clocked who it actually was, it is fair to say my mouth fell open. It was Viv Richards. My hero.

This was the guy along with Michael Holding who captured my imagination at The Oval in 1976 and made up my mind that I wanted to become a cricketer.

And here he was introducing himself to me.

'I hear you're a fast bowler with a good bouncer,' he said.

'Yeah, I've got a bit of pace, and I like making batsmen hop about,' came my reply.

The conversation went on from there and while I can't give you every word uttered some 40 years later, the most important thing that he said to me that day was this.

'You are a young Black man, and it will never be easy being a Black man trying to make your way, but you need to be strong. They are waiting for you to fuck up. They don't want to respect you and they want you to fail. Don't give them the satisfaction. Make them see you, make them respect you. Play the game as hard and as well as you can. You've got the skill and the ability to make it as a cricketer but you need to work hard to get there. Nobody is going to give you a thing so you have to earn it. Remember, don't give them the satisfaction of proving them right about you, use your cricket ability to prove them wrong.'

By the time our chat was over I felt about 10-feet tall. I was totally inspired and from that point on, I never looked back. It was a moment that changed my life. It was exactly what I needed to hear from exactly the right person and I will always thank not only Viv for that but Tony too for taking a chance on me.

For him to arrange this meeting with Viv was above and beyond, and it totally struck the right chord with me.

I sat there thinking, I'm this young kid from Gloucester, a nobody, and here I am getting this one-to-one advice from Viv Richards, the greatest cricketer in the game at that time and a guy who I just idolised. It was a bit surreal.

Viv and I have spoken about that meeting since and we have a laugh about it, especially because things came full circle about a decade later.

At The Oval in 1991, Viv was playing in his final Test match of a glittering career and was given the sort of reception to and from the crease deserving of a hero.

He was my hero and he had given me the focus that I needed, at a time I really needed it, but as he walked out to bat for the final time, I knew that I couldn't treat him any differently to any other batter.

I was in the England team that day playing in my third Test, trying to establish myself as an international bowler. I had played in the third Test at Trent Bridge where Viv had scored 80 in a nine-wicket win. I had seen up close just how good he was even at the end of his career and didn't have much success against him. Even in his final match he still had plenty in the tank to cope with most bowlers. His first boundary was a back-foot punch through the off-side off my bowling, and if I hadn't been the bowler I might even have appreciated the quality of the shot.

The West Indies were in a bit of trouble when he arrived in the middle and steadily he inched them towards a stronger position, threatening to make sure we had a stiff total to chase.

But just when he looked to be in complete control, he decided to take me on and try and hit me back over my head.

The only surprise came when he hit the ball off the inside edge of the bat and rather than sail towards the ropes it was directed straight to Hugh Morris at mid-wicket, who took the catch. I was pleased as punch to get the wicket and help my team, but to get Viv out for the very last time in international cricket was something I will always treasure.

Most people won't know just what an impact he had on my life all those years beforehand, but whenever I see the scorecard that says Richards ct Morris b Lawrence 60, it means so much more than just another Test wicket. Simply put, I don't think I would have made it as far as I did without his encouragement.

The same, I should add, must be said of Tony Brown. He stood firm behind me when others would have saved themselves the bother and acquiesced to those at the club who wanted me gone.

Tony saw something in me that not everybody did. He saw potential and he saw excellence and he wanted me to make the most of what I had. Without him I'd have been sacked, no doubt about it.

You need people like that in your life, who are prepared to go that extra mile for you and who are prepared to give you a second or third chance when you need it.

I can't imagine how many young lads were denied that chance in the game due to some small misdemeanour just because they didn't have anyone backing them up.

Tony wasn't the only person who did that for me, but there were plenty too who were quite happy to try and tear me down. They didn't win though, and I like to think that, in the end, I did Tony and Viv proud.

In fact I know that Viv was pleased with the way things turned out for me because he wrote some very kind words about me in his own autobiography, which meant a lot when I first saw them.

More recently he sent me a video message that was played at a fundraising dinner at Bristol City's Ashton Gate stadium which was a highlight among some great messages.

He is still my hero and even in my wheelchair, I still felt 10-feet tall when I listened to him talking about me.

He reminisced about that final Test match where I got him out, but also the fact that when we met in the odd West Country derby between Gloucestershire and Somerset, I was a handful for him.

The reason for that is simply because I always raised my game against him. I always wanted to perform at my best and show him just how good I was and how much his influence on me had worked.

I had nothing but respect for Viv as a cricketer and a man. He was one of the very best to ever walk out to bat and more often than not he would have the upper hand.

But if you did well against him then you knew you had achieved something special. It was almost like getting a seal of approval from your older brother or mentor.

CHAPTER SIX

Racism and Cricket

I am finding myself getting increasingly frustrated at being able to do less and less for myself. Whether it is cutting up my food to eat or gripping things like cups and people's hands.

Those small gestures that we all take for granted are now becoming a real battle and a challenge that I am going to start losing shortly.

My body is getting weaker and weaker, and the great muscle definition that I worked so hard to achieve is disappearing before my eyes.

There is nothing I can do to stop it. No extra rep on the weights machine, no extra push up. My body is becoming a shadow of its former glory and when you have put in as much effort as I have, that is a body blow – excuse the pun.

I need to remember that the body is only part of who I am. It is what is inside that matters, which is something that we could all take on board, when it comes to how we treat each other.

In 2020 English cricket began what you might call a reckoning with racism in the game, or at least started to confront the issue in a more meaningful way than it had done before.

That is because Western cultures started to look a little more closely at just how racist they still were in the aftermath of the murder of the unarmed George Floyd in the USA.

The ripple effect of video footage of a policeman's knee being used to choke the life out of a man who repeatedly said 'I can't breathe,' was significant for a time and the conversation came to the forefront of every industry that was forced to look at itself and ask, 'Are we racist?'

Well I can tell you from first-hand experience that English cricket has long been littered with racists and apologists for racism, and it is far from unique in that regard.

I have had to deal with a variety of incidents and situations throughout my life, not just in the game, and that is the reality of being Black in a white society. It is simply a part of life and you have to find ways of dealing with it and coping with it so that it doesn't destroy you.

Sometimes you fight back, sometimes you call it out, sometimes you make a stand. But sometimes you do nothing. Sometimes you stay silent. Sometimes you cry.

My overarching view as a 61-year-old Black man is that you stand up for yourself and you call out racism wherever you see it. That has been my approach by and large and it is the only way to make it clear that racism is wrong. Full stop.

But I also know that it can be incredibly difficult to do so at times and I'm not proud to say that I have failed to do just that on occasions.

Back in 1980 I was playing my first game for the Gloucestershire second team and one evening I was in my hotel room when I got a knock at the door. I opened it to find that one of my teammates had left a banana skin there for me to find. It was a classic racist trope that was used to compare Black people to monkeys.

Black footballers would often have bananas thrown at them by fans and there is a wonderful photo of the great John Barnes back heeling one away from him with utter disdain and dismissiveness, showing that he was above such ridicule and had more skill in his foot than the perpetrator could ever hope to have.

I didn't have the wherewithal to flick the banana skin away, or to confront the person who had put it there. Instead I picked it up and put it in the bin and then sat on the bed wondering who would do such a thing and why? Obviously it was a racist act, even if it might be disguised as a 'joke' or 'banter' in an era when the jokes were almost always at the expense of the minority.

But why would a teammate of mine do this? Sports team dressing rooms are not for the faint-hearted and they were about as unreconstructed and as coarse as you can get in the 70s and 80s, but the mickey-taking and the wind-ups and the colourful language is all possible without abusing people for the colour of their skin, their hair, their religion, their heritage, or any other characteristic. It is just unnecessary.

Forty years ago, it went on and I was the butt of the 'joke'. And it hurt. I felt like there was nothing I could do about it. I just had to take it. I was still young and hadn't really worked out how I would handle things like this, because I was experiencing it for the first time. I wish I could tell you that I confronted the person who put it there and had it out with them and made them see the error of their ways, but I didn't. I wish I could tell you that I laughed it off and rose above it and used it as motivation for the game I was playing in, but I didn't.

I sat down on my bed on my own, as feelings of worthlessness and loneliness washed over me, and I cried. If this is the way that my own teammates see me, then what about those I'm playing against?

I managed to find out who had put it there and then continued to share a dressing room with them thereafter, but I didn't confront him. I just knew we wouldn't be friends.

The feelings of upset and shame were something that I was keen to avoid in the future and that is perhaps the one good thing to come from that first experience.

I was annoyed that I didn't do anything about it, and I was angry that anyone could see me as such a soft target. I had felt like a bit of a coward in the moment, I didn't know how to react really. I just closed the door and cried. From that moment on, I would not let anyone put me down like that without getting a reaction.

And that is why the winter of 1980 was when I changed my attitude both mentally and physically around this issue.

I promised myself that would never happen again and that winter I went to the local gym in Bristol, The Empire, where the Commonwealth gold medal weightlifter Precious McKenzie used to train, and worked so hard on transforming my body into one that was not only fit for purpose on the field but one that wouldn't be messed with off it.

I just went every day and trained myself so hard, I created a new person. And I said to myself, 'Nobody will ever mess with me again. If they do ,there will be consequences.'

I had been a shy kid, but I knew that was not going to be me any more. I wouldn't be walking into a room with my head down avoiding eye contact.

That was the way. If you were a Black kid and you walked into a room, you didn't dare say anything. You were shy and quiet and kept yourself to yourself. I made the decision that is not going to be me.

If I have to argue with everyone in the club then so be it, I will argue. But that is not going to be me any more.

People would have to think twice about coming for me because there might just be something stronger coming back in their direction.

And while that might seem rather basic and immature, it was a visible language that everyone could understand. I wasn't going to be someone to be messed with.

I wasn't going to quietly enter the dressing room and hide away in a corner any more. That wasn't really my personality, but over time you get taught that this is the way for young Black men to behave to avoid suspicion or to avoid having your collar felt.

It was a way to try and fit into environments where you didn't traditionally belong and a county cricket dressing room was certainly one of those places.

I had plenty of friends in that Gloucestershire side of the 1980s and early 90s, but I can't say that I got on with everyone.

While I was a little blindsided by the initial banana incident in the second team, as time went on I was more able to deal with situations and to work out which teammates I could get on with and who would be just colleagues.

And that is the same for any workplace. People think that a cricket or sports team is different because you are playing games together and that is a fun thing to do. And most people play sport with their friends so it is natural to think that the same is the case at the professional level, but it is still just a job.

And I was happy to play alongside and work towards the same goal with people I didn't see eye-to-eye with. That's ok. We don't all have to get on with each other all the time, and I'm ok with that. I don't need everyone to be my friend.

I would prefer to get on with you, and I'm not going to be antagonistic for the sake of it, but if we don't see eye-to-eye on something, I'm happy to agree to disagree.

I had a couple of teammates over the years who had some right-wing views that didn't sit too well with me and they didn't really hide them at times, especially when they had had a few drinks.

On one occasion I actually got a call from a friend of mine who worked on the door of a bar in Bristol and he told me: 'We just had a guy down here who plays for Gloucestershire with you.' He told me his name and I said, 'Yes we were teammates'.

'Well, we've just had to knock him out,' came the reply. 'He was pissed and came to the door and we said you can't come in. He turned around and said, 'Why can't I come in you Black bastard?' At which point the guy on the door knocked him out. The ambulance came and treated him and they chucked him out as well, because he was so rude.' I would like to say that came as a surprise but it didn't. I didn't associate with this player much, but I felt the need to confront him and have a chat, because we were sharing a dressing room and he was a senior player.

I asked him about it and he said it was the drink talking and that is not how he saw me or the other Black players in our squad. He said it wouldn't happen again and that was that.

Naturally I remained unconvinced of his sincerity around this issue and kept my guard up.

But these were the sort of things that were regularly swept under the carpet and you just had to find a way to deal with them as a Black cricketer.

A couple of seasons into my career I might still have had a lot to learn in so many ways, but I was starting to find my voice on this subject thanks to my experiences.

I can remember there being a fixture arranged for the Gloucestershire seconds against an overseas side when I was about 19. I found out that it was a whites-only South African side playing under a bogus name in the middle of apartheid. Well there was no way I was going to be a part of these shenanigans. I went to see Tony Brown and told him that I wouldn't be playing in the game because they were trying to hide who they were. My principles would not be compromised on this and I told him so. To his credit, he said if I didn't want to play then he would respect that and it was my decision.

There would be more issues around South Africa and the club during the rebel tours, but this was one decision I was happy to make.

As I continued to develop as a cricketer I started to get mentioned for higher honours and that was something I was very happy to talk about in the media or to friends and supporters. That was always the ambition, to one day play for England.

But whenever I did well and then maybe did an interview where it was brought up, without fail I would receive a few letters as a result.

You might think or hope that they would be letters of encouragement from Gloucestershire fans who wanted to see one of their own make it to the top of the game, but not always.

In amongst the messages of support and goodwill, of which there were plenty, and I have always been very grateful for them, there would be letters like this.

Dear David,

I was watching the news and saw you talking about one day playing for England and representing your country.

Well it isn't your country. Who the f**k do you think you are you black ******? You've got no right to play for England, you need to go back to the f***ing jungle and play there.

How dare you say that you want to play for England. I don't want you playing for England you black *******. You and your kind will never be English.

Yours sincerely

Getting these letters in amongst some very nice ones from genuine fans was always a little shock to the system that someone would take the time to write their hate and their abuse down in a letter and then mail it to you. This wasn't an angry outburst because you had just been hit for 16 in an over or because you had lost a game. This required patience and thought and expense. These had to be well-held beliefs because it takes time to write a letter and to then get up and mail it. All that effort just to let someone know that you hate the colour of their skin.

The same goes on today of course, in a different format. Usually on a social media platform, by people hiding behind fake accounts and IDs. But it has the same effect. It might be easier to fire off abuse online, but the effect can be just as tough. No-one likes to be abused, and it doesn't matter what form it takes.

I've received letters and emails abusing me, and but nothing shook me quite as much as the day I spent playing for Gloucestershire against Yorkshire in 1984 in a Sunday League match at Scarborough.

It came in the middle of a Championship match we had started in Bradford the day before and it was a scorching hot day by the coast.

Away from the usual home ground of Headingley, it was a festival fixture and the ground was packed to the rafters.

Yorkshire had a strong side with the likes of Geoffrey Boycott and David Bairstow in the team and they didn't lose too many matches.

We batted first and scored 228-6 in our 40 overs, which wasn't a bad score at all back in those days, and I enjoyed watching our batters do a decent job without having to think about getting my pads on.

That was the last thing I enjoyed that day though as the afternoon turned into my worst experience on a cricket field.

I opened the bowling, and in the first over Boycott was run out for two, much to the disappointment of the home crowd. They had come to see their favourite son pile on the runs and take his team to victory. Sport doesn't work like that though.

Upset at Boycott's dismissal and with the sun beating down, I headed towards the long-leg boundary to field and I just hit a torrent of abuse.

'You Black b*****d! You n****r! Go home! F*** off back to Africa!…' And plenty more besides.

It was horrific, and it was relentless.

With the abuse also came bananas being thrown at me and this went on all afternoon. I couldn't believe how much anger and vitriol was coming out of their mouths.

We had another Black player in our side, John Shepherd, who played for Gloucestershire and for Kent and is a great man.

He was a bit older than me and he took me under his wing when I first came into the side and he too was being abused for the colour of his skin during the game.

He was upset, as I was, but he had experienced it before and was prepared to just ignore it and together we tried to support each other through the day.

I'm not a shrinking violet and by the age of 20, as I was then, I had already experienced racist abuse, but this was by far the worst and the most sustained I had ever come across. I felt awful.

And everyone knew it was going on. You couldn't not notice it and it got coverage in the press as a result.

I'm not sure what would happen if that sort of thing occurred now, but there would be an outcry and maybe the team would walk off the field as a couple of football teams have done.

What could I do though? At one stage my captain David Graveney tried to shield me from the abuse by bringing me into the ring to field, but that didn't stop them. So confident were they that there would be no repercussions, they carried on with the abuse and I had to stand there listening to it all afternoon.

It was just awful, and unlike the 90 minutes that footballers had to endure, this went on for three hours and I just couldn't avoid it.

Even when I was fielding closer to the middle there were times when the ball was hit past me and I had to give chase towards the boundary. I remember running after the ball and sounds of the monkey noises just got louder and louder with the odd expletive thrown in for good measure. It was a horrible day.

You can't concentrate on the job you're trying to do because you're constantly thinking about the abuse and trying to shut it out.

The next day we were back in Bradford to continue the Championship game and Bairstow came into our dressing room to have a chat before play.

He apologised for the behaviour of the Yorkshire fans who had abused me and promised me that it wasn't a view shared by the players and they were disgusted with it.

I took that on board but then asked what would be done as a result of it, after all these were their fans and it was their club, so something should be done.

Nothing was done, and the abuse continued.

I went back there in 1991 to play on that ground for the second and last time in my career and this time I was there as an England cricketer.

Just five days earlier I had been playing for England against West Indies at Trent Bridge and now I was back at the scene of one of my worst days.

I didn't enjoy being back there one bit. The memories of that day in 1984 came flooding back as I got to the ground and I wondered whether it would be just the same this time around.

I also made up my mind that if it was I was going to do something about it. I wasn't going to come to entertain this crowd and be abused for the effort.

I was also fairly confident I would do well on the field, because after that game I often raised my performance against Yorkshire because subconsciously I wanted to prove a point. And I think a few of the Black fast bowlers in the game did the same thing because it was the best way to respond to any negativity. I had a look at my figures against them and a year later in 1985 I took five wickets in the innings, and then in 1986 I took another five wickets in an innings.

And so to this game in 1991, I went out to bat in the first innings and was desperate to get something out of the middle. I managed to do just that and cracked a quickfire 38 not out which was my highest limited-overs score at the time and ended up being my best.

It took us to 209-6 from our 40 overs and as I made my way off the pitch, I noticed some of the abuse coming my way.

It was par for the course at Scarborough after my previous experience there, but this time there was a bit more pushback from others.

As the bananas started to appear, Yorkshire physio Wayne Morton dived into the crowd to confront the racists and was hauled out by the police who were trying to keep things calm.

It was at this point that a punter managed to get to me by the side of the pitch and confront me.

'Lawrence you Black b******!' he said. At which point I was ready to swing for him, but Darren Gough managed to intervene and just in time too as he came between us and stopped me from taking matters into my own hands. I wasn't a naive 20-year-old any more.

Goughie and I have talked about that incident since and we have a bit of a joke about it, but I was ready to go for that idiot, and probably it would have been me that got in trouble.

I got into the dressing room and I was seething. I might not have been on the end of the level of abuse I'd got seven years earlier, but nothing had changed. I was still seen as fair game for racist abuse from the Yorkshire fans.

With a few runs under my belt and fired up following that altercation, I came out and charged in as hard as I could to show what I could do with the ball.

As it had been in previous matches, the motivation was strong and I used it in the right way to take 4-27 in the game and help my team to a win.

That was the most satisfying part of that day, although if I had managed to knock out that fan it might have come a close second.

These incidents were part of my life experience and have added up to the person I am now. I think they do shape you and make a difference to how you react and deal with things. They have an impact on how you see the world and how you view your place in it.

CHAPTER SEVEN

Australia

Having played a handful of second XI games in 1980 and a few more the following summer, I made my County Championship debut in a one-off game against Glamorgan in 1981, and it wasn't the dream start that everyone hopes for.

It was a home game in Bristol, which was great because it meant my mum and dad could get along to watch between their shifts. And they were so proud of me getting into the Championship first team for the county aged just 17.

I was delighted too, but if I thought I was ready to set the world on fire with the next step up in my career I was quickly disabused of that thought with my efforts on what was a very flat pitch.

Across two innings I bowled 19 overs and took precisely zero wickets for 86 runs.

Not exactly an eye-catching start for a strike bowler, but it was a good lesson to learn from the outset.

You are going to have more bad days than good as a professional sportsperson and you need to find a way to cope with that and make sure that when things go well you make the absolute most of it.

The next couple of seasons were a little bit up and down for me with injuries playing their part as well as my own youthful exuberance causing me a few problems here and there.

I didn't actually play any Championship cricket in 1982 as I continued to make my way in the second XI until injury curtailed my season in early August.

In 1983 I was given more opportunities to play but I really struggled to find any rhythm whatsoever and even though I had my pace, the radar was all over the shop.

I played eight Championship matches for Gloucestershire that season and took just seven wickets. It was a huge disappointment.

There was a lot of chat around the club about the need to freshen up the bowling attack because we had become the whipping boys of the Championship and we didn't really have much pace in our ranks at all.

The hierarchy at the club were aware of the potential availability of a young West Indian quick bowler who had caught the eye on a youth team tour of England in 1982. His name was Courtney Walsh. Our coach Graham Wiltshire had been introduced to him and Walsh showed some interest, but he was still young.

He signed for Tynedale CC in Northumberland in 1983 where he helped them win their league title for the third season running, and the club were reminded of his quality by the father of our opening batter Paul Romaines.

Paul's dad had watched him play for Tynedale and spoke very highly of him. He also turned out for a couple of representative sides and showed he could mix it against the best, dismissing Graham Gooch for a Northumberland and Durham side against an International XI in an exhibition match.

Courtney hadn't played for West Indies yet, but he'd been showing what he could do for Jamaica in the Caribbean first-class competition and with so many West Indian overseas players in English cricket, word had got around about him.

Courtney had actually signed for a second season with Tynedale in 1984, but Northamptonshire were ready to buy him out of that contract and bring him to Wantage Road.

Thanks to that initial approach from Graham, Courtney believed he should speak to Gloucestershire first, which proved to be a lucky move on Graham's part.

Another thing to consider was that West Indies were touring the UK in 1984 and there was every chance that he would be a part of that squad.

Once it was selected, Courtney's name was included and that meant he wouldn't be available to the club in the Championship until after the tour was over.

But while his debut against Worcestershire at the back end of August is registered as his first-class debut for the club and his first appearance in county cricket, he actually opened the bowling for Gloucestershire with me before that.

At the start of May, and a couple of weeks before the Windies tour had got underway, Courtney came to Taunton and then to Worcester to play for Gloucestershire Under-25s in two one-day games to get himself ready for the tour. He only took a couple of wickets but we were all excited to see how he would go against England and then play alongside him when he joined us again.

As for the two of us, we hit it off immediately. He and I became firm friends over the years but it started that first day in Taunton and boy did we have some fun thereafter.

I kept an eye on how he was doing throughout the tour, and although he played plenty of cricket, he couldn't find a way to push past Joel Garner, Malcolm Marshall and Michael Holding into the Test side. His time would come soon after.

Once the tour was done he returned to us and we got on with the back end of the season, trying to lift what had been a pretty dismal campaign.

Despite his efforts, we stayed rooted to the bottom of the table with just one win from 24 games. No fun for anyone.

I remember thinking that this was quite a pivotal moment for the club because the next season we would have Courtney throughout, and having taken 41 wickets, I felt that I needed to kick on to the next level.

I had told Courtney that I was looking for a challenge over the winter and that I wanted to go to Australia and try to play some cricket over there. He was happy to hear that as he knew he was going to be over there with the Windies so he suggested we meet up if I got it sorted.

I made some enquiries at the club to see whether it might be possible. I wanted to play in Australia because I'd heard it was a good place for quick bowlers to bowl and especially in Perth where they had fast and bouncy pitches and where some of my cricketing heroes were from. I loved Dennis Lillee and thought he was a great example of a fast bowler, and then there was Lennie Pascoe as well who was as quick as they come on his day.

Calls were made on my behalf and I was set up with a chance to play grade cricket over in Western Australia at a club called Scarborough. That was a name that would mean two very different things to me following my experience against Yorkshire.

I didn't really know what to expect over in Australia. I'd never been on a long-haul flight before and here I was flying over to Perth to broaden my cricket experience.

It was eye-opening for me as a Black man in a country where the dark-skinned indigenous community were shunned and utterly disregarded as people. Things have changed a lot since then. I was watching the start of the Rugby League season recently and they had an indigenous team playing against an all-star team and it was a real celebration of Aboriginal and Torres Strait heritage and culture. I thought how good it was that they were not only being recognised but celebrated.

When I was there in 1984 they were treated as though they were worthless. A regular refrain would be something like: 'Don't worry about the Abos mate, they are just drunks.'

The way they were treated shocked me and made me wonder whether things actually weren't so bad in Britain.

I was 20 years old and still very naive about the world. Only six months earlier I had seen a music video for a song by David Bowie that featured indigenous people in Australia, dancing and strolling around the city, and I thought, 'That looks like fun'. How wrong I was. Life for most of the indigenous people that I came across was not much fun in those days.

What I did understand was how oppression was easily exported around the world, and it didn't matter whether you were the original inhabitants of a place, or had been invited to help rebuild that place, or had even been born in that place, if your face didn't fit with those who held power, then you were in trouble.

And far too often it is the people with brown and Black faces who are marginalised and oppressed. That is just a fact of this world and I think about it a lot.

In a previous chapter I talked about my relationship with race and racism and how it is something that I have tried to rail against and call out where possible throughout my life.

But the reality is that I am not going to solve racism and you pick and choose your battles.

Going to Australia in 1984, I admit I did little to alter the status quo, and the fact that I wasn't treated in quite the same way as the indigenous population meant that I was able to enjoy my time in Perth.

What I got was the opposition singing, 'Day-O, me say Day-O. Daylight come and me wanna go home,' as I made my way to the wicket for my first innings for the club.

They were not trying to make me feel welcome by singing a calypso song, I know that much. And the volleys of abuse that came thereafter were lively and sustained, but they were mostly about my Englishness rather than the colour of my skin, so while I didn't particularly enjoy it, I didn't often react. Occasionally it would veer towards the subject of race, and I would fire back, but it never went beyond words.

This was Australian club cricket and I didn't realise how tough it was over there. I'd played club cricket in England, a load of second-team games and quite a few first-team games by this stage, but none of it was like the way grade cricket was played in Australia. These guys were in your face, swearing at you, snarling and spitting near you, trying to wind you up in every kind of way. It was tough, hard cricket. And on the field I loved it. I had a fantastic time, bowled well, took wickets and my teammates were great and treated me as one of their own.

And so in one sense I really liked the Aussies and the Aussie culture because they played the game hard and then once the match or the day was over they would be the first to come and have a beer with you. They would abuse the hell out of you on the field and then have a laugh and a joke with you and talk cricket after play in the clubhouse and I liked that.

I appreciate that times have changed and there is no way that players in Australia or anywhere else would get away with saying the sort of things they did back then, and that is a good thing.

But the general interpretation of what was acceptable in the mid-80s was different to what it is now. And as an often lone Black face at a cricket ground, what was I going to do if things crossed a line?

In my first game for the club we played against a team that included Nigel Felton from Kent. We became firm friends. After the game, we were having a chat in the pavilion and I asked him what he was up to during his time in Perth, and he explained that he had come over with his wife and they were in the process of looking for somewhere to live for the summer. I had been given a two-bedroom apartment by the club to use during my stint and so I suggested that maybe he would like to move in with me and we could split the rent and make it a much better time for all of us.

He and his wife Jill came round and had a look and they decided to go for it. They moved in and for the next six months we had a great time living together, playing cricket and enjoying ourselves. Jill was brilliant, great fun, and she looked after us with some brilliant home-cooked food that allowed us to concentrate on our cricket.

I got on really well with Felts and it just worked brilliantly. We never had a cross word. We did a few different jobs while we were out there, like coaching and labouring.

But I also found myself earning extra money in the late-night economy.

One day I was on the beach and this guy introduced himself and said that he owned a local nightclub and wondered if I was looking for any work.

I said I was interested, but asked what sort of work it was. He said they were looking for waiters, and they wanted to hire good-looking men with good physiques.

That brought a smile to my face immediately. Who doesn't want to be told someone thinks they are good looking?! So I was still interested, and then came the kicker.

'We want waiters who are comfortable with themselves and have confidence in their bodies because there will be quite a few women in our club, and our staff don't have many clothes on...'

'What do you mean? What do they wear?' I asked.

'The uniform is pretty simple, it is just two items... a bow tie and a G-string, and the money is seriously good.' I chuckled at that and thought, 'I'm going to be a Chippendale'. I took the details and told the owner I'd let him know if I was still interested in a couple of days.

When I went back to the apartment, I thought that Felts and Jill wouldn't be that impressed by my latest job offer.

But when I told them, neither of them said not to do it. Felts immediately asked, 'Is the money any good?' And when I said it was, he thought I should do it, and Jill said she thought the ladies would be delighted.

That was all the encouragement I needed, and the next day I found the club and spoke to the owner and thus began my career as a (semi) naked waiter for three months. It was great fun, and the money was good thanks to the tips.

I must stress I didn't do anything untoward and it all stayed just the right side of fun. The customers and the staff were great and I think I spent more time laughing and smiling in that job than I had in any other up to that point.

Back at the cricket club things were going really well for me and I learnt so much from my time there.

I really improved as a cricketer thanks to the games I played but also the coaching I received while I was there from former Aussie international cricketer Mick Malone.

He knew so much about the game and I was able to pick his brains throughout that season and pick up lots of information that stayed with me for years afterwards.

For a lot of young players a winter playing overseas can be the making of them and I think that was the case for me because when I returned to Gloucestershire for the 1985 summer I was unrecognisable.

I was fitter, leaner, stronger and, dare I say it, more mature than when I left, and it showed in my cricket the next year.

The quality of the cricket was seriously good. At times I think their A grade would easily be comparable to county cricket and it was based on pure competition. Young players were desperate to make it into their state side and there was a real connection and pathway from club cricket to state and then international cricket.

If you performed in grade cricket you could get noticed and be promoted through the ranks quite quickly. It was anything but a closed shop, it was a very clear environment of opportunity and I liked that.

That competition is what helped me to improve my cricket, and because the games were played across two weekends, when it was your turn in the field you had to work bloody hard for your wickets.

Batters might only get one chance to bat in four weeks so when they got in they really made you work, and on those blazing hot days you get in Perth it was seriously hard graft.

But that is what cricket at the highest level is about and I was never afraid of getting my hands dirty and bowling the tough overs when things weren't going our way.

I do think the experience stood me in good stead for what was to come and it should still have a role to play in the development of young players at the start of their professional careers. It has helped so many players, and I know guys like Alec Stewart, Paul Collingwood and Stuart Broad have all spoken about how their time in Australia playing grade cricket made a difference to them.

But you have to go with the right attitude and with a willingness to give it everything on and off the field. It is not just an excuse to get on the lash in the sunshine. I look back on that winter so fondly even now, and I was really made to feel like part of the club.

* * *

My birthday is on January 28, shortly after Australia Day on January 26.

Now I know that this date is controversial because it recognises the arrival of the first British Fleet in 1788 to Sydney Cove, which is the beginning of both the development of Australia as the nation we know today and the marginalisation of the First Nations people who are still fighting for equality today.

Back in 1985, I was told that it was a celebratory bank holiday weekend and there was no cricket to play. One of my teammates, Crawford, knew it was my birthday and invited me over to his family farm where we had a great weekend fishing and getting stuck into outdoors life.

While I was there, they invited all their friends from the local area to come round and they threw a party for my 21st birthday which was so special.

The dad then made a speech as though he was my dad, and he spoke about me in a really kind way which was so touching and really made me feel accepted.

I enjoyed my time there so much that I was keen to get back the following winter if I could, but my success on the field meant that I was selected for an England B tour to Sri Lanka at the start of 1986 so I couldn't play a full season in Australia.

The club wanted someone who could play throughout, so we agreed that I would try and find a short-term deal elsewhere, and so I ended up at Clarence District Cricket Club in Tasmania alongside Brian Davison. Originally from Zimbabwe, Brian had been a stalwart at Leicestershire during the 1970s, but had come and played a season for us at Gloucestershire, so I managed to get a couple of months of cricket for his grade team in Hobart.

Three years later I found myself back in Western Australia somewhat unexpectedly when I picked up a three-month gig to play for Fremantle District Cricket Club. It was unexpected because I had just made my Test debut that summer against Sri Lanka and was named on the Test tour to go to India that winter. But a diplomatic row prevented the tour from taking place and everyone was sent on their way to find other things to do. I had enjoyed Australia so much the last time that I wanted to head back there again, and this time as an international cricketer I was looked after even better with paid-for accommodation and a fee for playing as well. I only had to do a little bit of coaching and there was no need to do any waitering this time!

I had a good season with them and took plenty of wickets and I enjoyed it so much that in 1994 I decided to emigrate and move out there for good.

I had recently announced my retirement from cricket following my attempts to come back from a serious knee injury and was at a bit of a crossroads.

Gaynor and I had gone to a friend's party in Bristol and towards the end of the evening things ended up kicking off with a couple of guests who were being racially abusive. I was fed up with things like this. It might not have been as often as it was in the 70s or 80s but it was never too far below the surface and I was tired of it.

A few days later I said to Gaynor, 'Come on, let's go to Australia. Let's leave the UK and bring our son up in the sunshine and have a fresh start.' Gaynor was enthusiastic and we were absolutely committed to moving. Fremantle agreed to sponsor me and take me on to do some coaching while I looked for work, and I was confident I could make my way in Australia.

I would have had a great friend, George, Down Under too thanks to my earlier stint at Scarborough in 1984. I had stayed in touch with him during that winter, as we wrote letters to each other while he completed his electrical engineering apprenticeship.

I told him it was so good that he should come out and visit me the following winter and experience it for himself, and he did. I had already gone back home for the England B tour by the time he came out, but that didn't stop him. He travelled around Australia himself and had a great time. So much so that Australia became his home and he is now an Aussie citizen.

We were going to do the same thing and had got everything ready. We put the house on the market and had found a buyer and started winding things up and packing for the move. But just before we were about to leave, my father-in-law had a stroke and we had to change our plans.

We had to stay nearby to help and I'm glad we did because within four years Gaynor's father had passed away, and it was good that she had that time with him.

I do sometimes wonder what might have happened had we gone. I think we would have loved it and I'm sure Buster would have had a great time out there.

We might only have stayed for a few years or we might never have come back, but it is a shame we didn't get the chance to live out there as a family.

Life takes twists and turns that you don't expect and you have to be ready to adapt to whatever comes your way.

CHAPTER EIGHT

County and Courtney

Playing the sport you love for the place you're from is a huge privilege and one I hope I never lost sight of.

Even though I always wanted to play for England and set my sights on being the best I could be, pulling on the Gloucestershire shirt and performing for my county was always a big source of pride and one that I reflect very fondly on.

Even now as I find myself able to do less and less as my motor functions slowly grind to a halt, I can still think back in my mind to games and moments on the field that I remember to this day and it brings a smile to my face.

During my time at Gloucestershire we came so close to winning a first County Championship but sadly we never got over the line. Even more frustrating is that we still haven't come any closer than we did as runners-up in 1986.

That season we built on the success of 1985 with Courtney Walsh taking an unbelievable 118 first-class wickets and myself chipping in with 63, but we were denied the bowling skills of Kevin Curran, who played as a batter only during that summer due to injury.

He did well with the bat, scoring over a thousand runs and hitting four hundreds, but we really missed his bowling in the final tally.

The Championship was won by Essex, who had a brilliant side and won six titles in a stunning 13-year period from 1979.

We had some right ding-dong battles with them during the mid-80s, and in 1986 it was no different when we played them up at Castle Park in Colchester.

It was the back end of the summer so the pitches were dry and this was a game dominated by spin rather than pace. I only took two wickets in the game, although such was Courtney's class he still picked up a six-for in the first innings. Left-arm spinner John Childs took 8-58 to put Essex in control, but the thing that I remember is Essex's push for victory on the final day.

They had given themselves around 90 overs to try and bowl us out and take the win that would have made the title a formality, while we had to get a draw to stay in the hunt ourselves.

Unlike now there were no points for a draw, only the bonus batting or bowling points you scored. If the two sides had the same set of results in the current Championship then we would have won the title. But anyway.

The game was in its last throes and Essex were pushing hard for the win and they had us eight wickets down with all the men around the bat.

Our number three Phil Bainbridge had batted for almost the entire innings for a half-century, but he needed support.

With two overs to go our skipper David Graveney was caught by one of those close catchers and Essex were cock-a-hoop. The only thing between them and the win was the new batter… me!

I don't know why, but with the atmosphere as tense as anything, I decided to invoke my inner Viv Richards and strolled out to the middle with the biggest swagger I could muster. I wanted to show these Essex boys that I meant business and that this was the easiest job in the world for me to block out a few balls and see my team home.

There was a bit of chirp as there always was from them, but as I chatted to Phil, I rose above it. I stuck my chest out. I walked up and down the pitch doing a bit of 'gardening', as if I was Viv himself.

I asked for a middle-stump guard with my booming voice, full of confidence and dominating the space, and then for some strange reason, because I'd never done it before or since, I thought I would twirl my bat because guys that did looked supremely confident. Think of Alec Stewart. Instead of looking confident though, I managed to throw the bat into the air and then when I tried to catch the bat, it hit the floor and bounced away from me so I had to chase my own bat.

The Essex fielders were in hysterics and rolling around laughing, while I looked like a numpty. Any tension in the game had just disappeared. I managed to block out eight deliveries as we secured the draw and kept our hopes alive. My teammates were delighted and were patting me on the back as we walked back in, and then they promptly took it in turns to spin their bats and drop them. Something that carried on for a few weeks after the event.

If that was a moment where I felt the happiness of my teammates at a job well done, the following season I experienced the complete opposite.

We had a frustrating summer in the Championship, winning just five games and finishing 10th in the table. But in the one-day tournaments we performed reasonably well and perhaps should have captured some silverware before Mark Alleyne's Gloucestershire side brought sustained success in the shorter game from 1999 onwards.

In 1987 we reached the semi-finals of the NatWest Trophy but were blown away by Richard Hadlee's Nottinghamshire, who went on to win that year.

And we faced Kent in the quarter-final of the Benson & Hedges Cup in one of the most thrilling games I ever played in.

We got ourselves up to 250-7, which in those days was a competitive score. We would have to bowl well, but we fancied our chances.

As Kent's chase wore on, those chances looked increasingly slim and at 228-4 with five overs remaining, the game was theirs.

But a wicket can change everything. First I caught Graham Cowdrey in the deep, and soon after I dismissed his brother Chris caught behind.

They were still the favourites, but when Eldine Baptiste gave me another catch in the penultimate over, the equation became five required to win from the final over with three wickets in hand, and yours truly to bowl.

I managed to tease an edge from Chris Penn at the start of the over, leaving five still needed with their number 10 Daniel Kelleher walking to the middle. He was clearly uncomfortable and didn't lay a bat on the first two balls. From the next Steve Marsh tried to get to the striker's end but he was run out off a wide. So with three balls left in the game and four more runs required, England legend Derek Underwood, right at the end of his career, walked out at number 11. I managed to bowl two more dot balls with everyone jittery as anything, including the batters. One more ball to go with four needed. One more ball Syd, come on. Nothing silly. No wides.

I run in and bowl a good length ball on the stumps and somehow Underwood swings his bat and the ball goes flying over my head. Jeremy Lloyds is at mid-off and he makes a huge dive to try and stop it but it is just wide of him, and it continues to the boundary so Kent win the game by one wicket from the last ball. I'm sick.

Seconds ago I felt as alive as I have done on a cricket field, now everything has drained away from me and I cannot believe what has just happened. I've lost the game for my team. It is my worst moment on a cricket field at that point.

I walk into the changing room and say sorry to the boys, grab my stuff and then I walk out. Nobody tries to stop me. Everyone is just gutted at the result, and I'm sure in the heat of the moment they are disappointed with me. The room is quiet, sombre, and I leave without getting changed. There was only one person I could speak to at this point so I called my mum. I was in tears and I said to her, 'Mum I don't know what just happened. I've lost the game for the boys and it is all my fault'. She didn't know much about cricket, which is probably why I felt I could confide in her about things like this.

'Don't worry son, you did your best. Today just wasn't your day, and that is ok.' It is what I needed to hear.

Two days later we are playing in a benefit match, which was probably for the best because it allows everyone to get the game out of their system, and we have a few drinks and the guys are more encouraging to me, because we all know these things happen in cricket. It is just an awful feeling when they happen to you.

* * *

I've been fortunate to make some lifelong friends during my time as a cricketer and none more so than Courtney Walsh, who was the finest bowler I played alongside in my career and an equally fine man.

We got on well from the start, when our paths first crossed in an Under-25s game, and we are still great friends to this day.

Courtney has been supportive and has sent me messages since he first found out about my condition and they have meant a huge amount to me.

Our bowling partnership at Gloucestershire should have brought us a County Championship crown and I'm gutted that we didn't manage to get over the line, but we had great fun trying.

He was undoubtedly one of the very best to have ever played the game, and he was a bit of an inspiration for me as a teammate.

That started during my stint in Perth in 1984 where I got the chance to see him make his Test debut at the WACA alongside so many of my heroes from 1976.

Courtney very kindly sorted me tickets for each day of the Test and I was so excited to be able to watch West Indies once again up close. I watched them bat all day on day one and then missed day two because I was playing club cricket. But on day three the Windies bowlers put on a hell of a show. Michael Holding took six wickets to bowl Australia out for just 76, meaning Courtney didn't even get a bowl.

Clive Lloyd enforced the follow-on and in the second innings Courtney got his first Test wicket as part of a big innings win.He played in all five matches in a thumping 3-1 series win and his Test career was up and running.

We had a good catch up in Perth and had a few drinks after the game and promised to bring the heat back to Gloucestershire with us the next year, and that is exactly what we did.

The 1985 season was one of my most enjoyable campaigns because it was the first full season I played together with Courtney and Kevin Curran, who had also joined us. I was straining at the leash to get started and in my first Championship game I took nine wickets against Lancashire which got me up and running.

After his international duties, Courtney arrived in time for the third game of the season against Sussex and I was flying. I bowled like the wind and took 7-48 to get people's attention.

Sussex skipper John Barclay called it the fastest spell he had seen at Hove, while Courtney gave me a big pat on the back as we came off the field and thanked me for making life easy for him having just got off the plane. That was a big moment for me because all of a sudden I had people talking me up as a potential England player.

With Bob Willis having retired the previous summer, the hunt was on for England's next fast bowling star and I was making my move at just the right time. Two games later we played Derbyshire in Derby and up against Michael Holding I took another five wickets. Courtney took the other five as we bowled our side to victory on the last day.

That was a feeling I will never forget and it is one that we got to enjoy a fair few more times together over the years, but to do it nice and early was a great marker and it showed us just how potent a partnership we could be.

We bowled with real pace and with real intent too. When you came up against us as a batter, you had to be brave to score runs.

Guys like Allan Lamb, Robin Smith and Wayne Larkins were definitely in that category. 'Ned' Larkins in particular was a bit of a nemesis for me at Wantage Road. I didn't particularly like bowling there because I didn't get many wickets and Ned always seemed to hit me all over the place. Every bowler has a batter they struggle against and for me it was him.

The short ball was something we used to unsettle opponents so that when we pitched it up they would be hesitant and not quite in line which would mean we were more likely to find the outside edge. It was all about taking wickets.

But in that game against Derby, and then later on against Kent when Courtney and I shared seven wickets in the second innings, we were accused of intimidatory bowling.

It didn't bother us in the slightest. Whenever a team had a bowler with a bit of pace in the side they would use it to their advantage and we were no different. We were just lucky that with Courtney, myself and Kevin, the quick stuff just kept on coming. The aim was always to take wickets, not to hurt people. It was the threat of getting hurt that was the greatest weapon and that is what we used.

I took pleasure from seeing a batter jerk their head out of the way in surprise at how quick it was. Or if they ducked a bouncer and ended up on the floor, that was fine with me because it scrambled their minds and gave you more of a chance of getting them out.

Occasionally people did get hurt and had the bumps and bruises to show for the contest, but I always wanted people to remain healthy.

One day that wasn't the case and it was during a game against West Indies in 1988. They had all-rounder Phil Simmons opening the batting and he was a big imposing cricketer who could hit the ball a long way.

We were still in an era when helmets were not compulsory and lots of players didn't wear them, including Phil on this day.

I bowled him a bouncer with the new ball and as he went to duck it hit him on the head and he collapsed. It was a frightening moment but he got up, feeling worse for wear. I went over to check on him and make sure he was ok. He nodded, but he looked very shaky on his feet.

As he was helped from the ground by the team medic he collapsed again and this time he needed serious medical attention.

An ambulance came and took him to the hospital where he had life-saving surgery to relieve the pressure on his brain.

That was the day when all the West Indies players bar Viv Richards started to wear helmets against real pace and made sure they had them in their kit bags. As a bowler I didn't feel guilty about it because I was just doing my job and it was Phil's choice whether or not to wear a helmet. Obviously he was taking a risk by not doing so. As a human being, of course I felt for Phil, which is why the next day I went to visit him in hospital after he had the surgery and was recuperating.

I went into the room where he was lying down and his fiancée was sat there next to him and I just broke down in tears. I didn't want to have this effect on anybody. He motioned me over to him and as I stood there he took my hand and said, 'It's okay. It's not your fault.' I just felt so bad seeing him there wired up and I was the one who put him there. You don't play the game to do that.

There has always been an element of danger to the game and that is what makes it so thrilling. As a bowler you know that if a batter misses a short ball there is a chance that you could hurt them, but that is not going to stop you from trying to get them out any way you can. There is an understanding that the batter can also take advantage of that sort of delivery.

In the modern game every player wears a helmet so thankfully serious head injuries are more rare, but I think that batters might get hit in the head more than ever because they haven't had to learn how to evade the ball as much, and they are more prepared to have a hook at the ball knowing that they are protected. Either way I'm just glad that Phil was alright and able to continue his cricket career. He didn't play again on that tour understandably, but he was back on the field after three months and on the 1991 tour to England we faced off against each other again and this time it was in Test cricket.

Courtney and I had become good friends over the course of that first season and my dad loved chatting to him too as a fellow Jamaican when he came to watch my games. That Caribbean heritage brought us together too when it came to socialising and going out from time to time. We both enjoyed good music and a good party, although I was a bit more of a night owl than Courtney.

One thing we both had plenty of time for was the St Pauls Carnival that was held every summer so if you were an opposition batter and wanted a bit of respite from us, then you had to hope that we were playing you across Carnival weekend.

For some strange reason in the week leading up to the Carnival, my hamstring would get very tight and sore, and would you believe it, Courtney would also feel some stiffness in a similar area and would require some treatment.

It was either dumb luck or just an extraordinary coincidence that on around five occasions both Courtney and I would be out of action in the same game and have to stay at home resting our 'injuries'.Somehow those injuries would be enough to keep us out of cricket action, but we were just about fit enough to join the Carnival for the day before recovering in time for the next match.

It was amazing that no-one cottoned on to our regular little bit of cricketing truancy, but I guess no-one else had any interest in the event so we knew we were safe to enjoy ourselves without the club finding out, until now I guess.

Courtney was a gentle giant off the field, but he had his moments and he had a temper like anyone does when provoked. Most people were smart enough not to wind him up, but I can remember him losing his rag a couple of times.

There was a game against Derbyshire when Kim Barnett and Peter Bowler were batting and they were doing pretty well despite Courtney creating chances. A catch off Barnett was dropped and Bowler took exception to Courtney's mutterings. The next single he took, he bumped his shoulder into Courtney which set everything off and even had me steaming up from fine-leg to get involved. Bowler was waving his bat and Courtney was not happy and ready to rip the bat out of his hands. The umpires managed to calm things down, but Courtney was still reported for the incident.

Another time he had a run-in with one of his own teammates during a game against Hampshire.

The great Malcolm Marshall had come in to bat and there is no doubt that there was a lot of respect between him and Courtney. He would have been someone that Courtney looked up to and was learning from in the West Indies team, plus they were both fast bowlers so there was often a bit of an understanding between your fellow quicks.

But after bowling three half-volleys to Maco one of our team piped up and shouted, 'Come on Courtney, what's wrong with you?! How is it that you pitch it up to your lot, and to us blokes we get all the short stuff?!'

Everyone knew what he meant.

Maybe the teammate had a point in wanting to see the opposition given a tough time, but there was a way to do it which didn't involve shouting it across the ground for everyone to hear, calling into question Courtney's integrity as much as anything.

It took a while for everything to calm down after that, the player who made the comment apologised to Courtney afterwards, but the damage was done and they gave each other a wide berth after that. There were just some players you knew you were never going to see eye to eye with and the best thing was to give each other some space off the field. On it, we were still a team and we all pulled in the same direction in trying to help our side win.

Courtney was a proud Jamaican and I used to talk to him about life in Jamaica, a place where I had roots but hadn't visited. He told me about cricket at Sabina Park, which was one of the most famous and feared grounds in world cricket. Many a visiting batter would have nightmares about that place, and I made a promise to myself that I would get the chance to check it out.

The aim was clearly to be part of an England tour to the West Indies and to play a Test match on the island of my heritage, but after my knee injury in 1992, that aim had to be parked. I still wanted to experience the place though, and from the stories I had heard from Courtney and other players who had played there it was something that I knew I would enjoy. I just had this vision of sitting in the stands and watching a game unfold in the sunshine, with the noise of the crowd and with an ice cold Red Stripe in my hand. Doesn't that sound like bliss?

After returning to the Gloucestershire side in 1997, I had focused my attention on getting fit and firing for the 1998 season, but with England touring the Caribbean I thought this was my chance to make my pilgrimage and go and watch some cricket in Jamaica. I went out on my own as a supporter and stepped onto Jamaican soil for the very first time and couldn't have been happier.

I had arrived the day before the game and I was so excited to be there with the prospect of seeing so many of my friends on both teams playing in the match. The day of the game I was up a little later than I wanted due to jet lag, but I got myself sorted and jumped into a taxi and headed to the ground.

When I arrived the game was already in progress and England were batting. They had lost two wickets, which wasn't exactly a surprise since Curtly and Courtney had a habit of running through English top orders. I found out where my seat was and looked up at the scoreboard which read 7-2 at the end of the seventh over.

Before I settled in, I thought I'd better go and get that Red Stripe I had been looking forward to, but as soon as I got to the back of the stand I heard a huge roar of noise which I took to mean that England had lost another wicket.

Nasser Hussain was out and the two Surrey guys, Alec Stewart and Graham Thorpe, were in the middle. I had played in teams with both of them and I had also bowled to them and got them out, so I wanted to get back and see how they would cope with the Windies pace duo.

By the time I got back to my seat they were just finishing the 10th over and the score was 17-3. I took a sip of my beer and thought, 'This is great'. With two wickets already to his name to equal the tally of the great Dennis Lillee on 355 wickets, Courtney was at the top of his mark ready to bowl. I took another sip of the crisp, refreshing beer as he ran in and bowled a ball just back of a length to Thorpe, but it reared up and hit him on the glove, and he threw the bat down in pain and anger.

That wasn't a particularly unusual sight, to see batters find life uncomfortable against Courtney, but the ball had bounced much more steeply than Thorpey was expecting.

At this point, the players all gathered together in the middle, the umpires were involved, and then Mike Atherton, who had already been dismissed, came jogging out from the pavilion after the physio.

I didn't know what was going on. It all seemed a bit bizarre.

The next thing I knew, the players were walking off and the game was abandoned. I was stunned.

I turned to some fans next to me and asked what on earth was going on. 'It is a dangerous pitch, someone is going to get seriously hurt,' they said. What I didn't realise, having come into the ground 45 minutes after the start of play, was that the pitch was like a corrugated iron roof which meant if the ball bounced on the upslope it took off like a rocket, and if it landed on the downslope it would shoot along the floor like a pea-roller. And no batter in the world can cope with that kind of variable bounce.

The real worry was that Courtney and Curtly were two of the tallest fast bowlers in the world and the pace they bowled at made it seriously dangerous for the batters to face them.

You would be expecting the ball to bounce around your thigh or your hip, and suddenly it would be at your head. I knew what it was like to be the bowler who caused a serious head injury from bowling after what happened to Phil Simmons, and neither Courtney nor Curtly wanted to be the guy who did something similar to the England batters.

I spoke to Courtney afterwards and he admitted it was really difficult to keep running in and trying to bowl your best ball knowing that the pitch could make something awful happen. He didn't enjoy that hour of cricket and the right decision was made to abandon the match.

But it meant that my dream visit to Jamaica at the age of 34 to watch some Test cricket lasted precisely one ball. That is a hell of a long journey just to see one live delivery. They reconfigured the tour and ended up playing another match in Trinidad to make up for the abandonment, but I couldn't follow them there. I had to get home and prepare for the new English season, which unbeknown to me at that stage would be my last as a professional cricketer.

CHAPTER NINE

England B and A

During the 2024/25 winter I have been sure to stay nice and warm in the house, with the heating on and my blankets to cover me. Since I'm not moving around much, I am not generating anywhere near the heat I used to and so if I'm not careful I start to feel the cold very easily.

And when I do, I'm reminded how different this is to some of the conditions that I found myself in as a fast bowler, generating heat as I ran in to bowl in some of the hottest places on earth.

February 1986 was a case in point. Touring Sri Lanka with England B was swelteringly hot and bloody hard work, not helped by the fact that apparently there was no such thing as lbw unless the ball shot along the ground on middle stump. If you hit them on the pad, just return to your mark, you were never going to get a decision go your way. You had to hit the wickets. There is a reason why the international game eventually switched to neutral umpires – no nation had a blemish-free record on that score. Understandably the Sri Lankan umpires wanted their players to do well because they had only recently acquired Test status, winning their first Test match against India in 1985. Their second victory would soon follow against Pakistan in a series that overlapped with our tour. They played us in three first-class matches and they put out really strong teams, especially in the first game with six Test players including Arjuna Ranatunga playing.

All three 'Test' matches were played over four days rather than five, and the series was drawn 0-0, which is a reflection of the flat and unresponsive surfaces we played on.

It was hard work in oppressive heat and humidity. Because of that humidity, it would take me all of three balls to work up a sweat, and by the time I came off the field every piece of kit and clothing was sopping wet.

Even my boot laces were soaked. I would take them off and wring them out and watch the sweat hit the floor.

It was the hottest place that I ever had to bowl and, as a 22-year-old, I used to charge in like an idiot and bust as much of a gut in Colombo as if I were bowling in Bristol.

Perth is very hot too, but it's a dry heat so you feel like you can catch your breath, and since most of my games were on the coast there used to be a lovely breeze that would cool you down. In Sri Lanka it is so humid that you feel like you're drowning. But that didn't stop me. I kept running in and giving it everything I had because that is what my teammates and my captain always got from me.

I did wonder at times, though: why on earth have they sent me here? These are the flattest and toughest pitches for a fast bowler to bowl on.

My pace was my greatest asset and it was nullified by the pitch and the broad bats of the Sri Lankan batters. I found it hard to hurry the batters, especially when I pitched the ball short. There really wasn't a lot to get excited about. It was the complete opposite to the previous winter in Western Australia where a good length ball takes off and is caught above the keeper's head. In the first 'Test', I kept pounding in for over after over, searching for wickets and finding as much success as a fisherman in a desert.

I was young and I had enthusiasm, but this kind of work was enough to make any bowler feel old and tired. As I walked off the field at the end of that match having bowled 39 overs and ended up with figures of 0-147, I wondered what was the point?

I'd worked so hard and got absolutely nothing to show for it. How was that fair? When anyone looked at the scorecard all they would see is that I didn't get any wickets. They wouldn't have any idea how hard I worked for those figures.I turned to my teammate Derek Pringle and said, 'This is a stupid game, Pring! You bust your guts out there and get nothing for it. The scorebook never says how hard you try.' He just smiled back at me and nodded and said, 'Yes, you're right Syd, it doesn't'. That's the game we play and yet still we come back for more.

I took seven wickets across the entire tour at an average of 75, which is pretty ropey whichever way you look at it. But boy did

I earn each and every one of those seven! That trip was my first England representative tour and by the time I got another chance I had already made my full England debut and the name of the second team had been changed to England A.

I had been denied the chance to tour with England in 1988 due to a diplomatic stand-off between India and the rebel tourists so I was glad for the chance to go and play some cricket overseas again. It was the misfortune of Ricky Ellcock with the senior side in the Caribbean that gave me my chance because I hadn't originally been selected in the tour party. Chris Lewis was promoted to replace Ricky and I got a last-minute spot to replace Chris in the A squad.

This time the trip was to Zimbabwe and Kenya and my roommate was Mike Atherton. He and I got on pretty well even if we had some robust discussions around music. I can remember one in particular when I was playing Tracy Chapman and Athers wanted to talk to me about how radical she was.

He had just finished university and had lots of ideas about things and I was happy to talk. We also discussed Nelson Mandela because early on that tour he was released from prison. It was a hot topic of conversation and we were so close to it that journalists who had been sent to cover our tour were diverted to South Africa to cover Mandela's release instead. Fair enough I suppose.

Athers and I spoke about it and we both agreed how good it would be if we could go and listen to Mandela speak in person. It was only just over the border and we asked the management if it would be possible to go, but we were told we couldn't.

To be in Africa when Mandela was released was just brilliant though. You could really feel what a seismic moment it was. For a Black political prisoner to be freed by the apartheid South African government after so many years of oppression and brutality was just incredible, and I did feel closer to it in every way.

Our only brush with political power came when Zimbabwe president Robert Mugabe came to visit one of our matches and we were all introduced to him. I don't recall many of us being particularly enthusiastic about that visit though.

Athers had to meet him a second time when he was captain on the 1996 tour and Mugabe knew a good photo opportunity when he saw one. I think you can tell from the picture how uncomfortable

Athers was. We had a good tour together and he was a player I really admired throughout his career because he had plenty of skill but also had lots of character. He was a brave batter. He took on the fastest bowlers and had his fair share of success against them.

I hadn't seen him for a long while, but he came over to see me when I was at T20 Finals Day at Edgbaston in 2024 and he was working for Sky Sports. We had a good chat about our playing days and that tour, and he brought with him a squad photo from the trip which helped jog our memories.

He reminded me of one incident in Mutare where I had to take matters into my own hands when dealing with some so-called 'fans'. We had just finished the day's play and a rather gruff-looking Zimbabwean farmer who had been enjoying the grog and shouting various comments at the players decided that he wanted to continue the conversation in the dressing room.

Of course that is not a place for any punter to stroll into, and certainly not uninvited. But this guy barged past the young black lad on security, giving him a volley of racial abuse as he went.

We were all unimpressed and asked him to leave. The young lad tried to usher him out of the dressing room, but he turned on the steward and started to hit him. I wasn't going to stand for that kind of behaviour so I grabbed a hold of this bloke, put him in a headlock and all but carried him out of the pavilion. I threw him into the hedge outside, much to everyone's amusement.

It was my first visit to Africa and I was keen to experience it and see for myself some of the things Kevin Curran had told me about it, from the beautiful landscape to the wildlife, as well as the love that the locals have for their sport.

One night we were in a bar in Harare and a woman came up to me and said, 'Can you talk for me please? I want to hear you talk?' I wasn't quite sure what she was getting at to begin with, so I asked why. 'Oh, we've never heard a posh Black man talk before. Can you talk for us?' I wasn't about to be a performing seal for her, so in my broadest Gloucester accent I said: 'No, I don't think so. I'm not posh.' Unfortunately that only had the effect of her wanting to hear more, and I wasn't in the mood to put on a show.

Even in a place where you think the colour of your skin will not be an issue, where you won't be seen as an oddity or curiosity because most of the population are Black, there is still a way for you to be set aside as different.

The only time I can think of where something like this might happen the other way round is when people hear white Jamaicans speak for the first time. I can remember when I heard a white Jamaican talk in the thickest Caribbean accent, and I just loved it. I didn't ask for them to talk specifically for me though. I thought that would be rude.

This trip also happened to be Graham Thorpe's first England representative tour. He was a fantastic player and a good tourist too. He fitted into the group so well and was well-liked by everyone, so it was unbelievably sad to hear that he had taken his own life in 2024. He was a bit younger than me and is a true legend of the game. Whatever led to him making make that decision is personal to him. What I do know is that it brought up some questions for me as I was in the process of planning my own funeral as he had his.

I have been forced to study my own mortality far sooner than expected, and after receiving the diagnosis, there have been plenty of thoughts about how I might be able to make the same decision, because I don't want to wait until I am so frail that I am just a shell.

Those thoughts have filled my mind, but as I write they have been pushed away for now. Part of my life living with MND is about making decisions for when I am gone, and laying down a funeral plan is part of that.

The biggest decisions are around what music will be played of course. I'm happy with my selection, but the choices could have been at least 10 times greater, such is my love of music. But no-one wants to be listening to my playlist all day!

CHAPTER TEN

England Duty

My voice is weakening significantly now and I am struggling to lift up my arm to do things like wipe my nose or feed myself. It is a gradual but unrelenting diminishing of my powers.

I was told that the disease could be slow moving and I might stay at a certain level of movement for a while, but it hasn't been quite like that. I am still hopeful that I will be able to stretch things out for as long as possible, but the mere act of living has become the greatest trial yet.

I require help with my breathing through a machine during the night, just to get enough oxygen into me to help sustain me through the day. Soon I will need to have it during the day to help me breathe. I keep thinking back to the days when I would be training at the gym or playing for Gloucestershire and running in to bowl.

These are the memories that sustain me when I try to move my legs and see nothing but stillness and stiffness.

Was it all a dream? Did I really play cricket for England in front of thousands of people, who cheered when I took a wicket?

* * *

As a professional cricketer, playing for your country is always the dream. For most of us it starts before we really understand what being a sportsperson is all about. It is in the games that you play with your mates in the park or at school when you are pretending to be the stars of the time.

You're playing football and you call out the names of Cyrille Regis or Laurie Cunningham, or you're playing cricket and you call out Michael Holding or Ian Botham. And you imagine yourself on the biggest stage playing for your country and taking in the applause and adulation from the crowd. Then you're back in the classroom and the dream is pushed to the back of your mind once more.

Once you start playing the game a little more seriously then that thought of making it all the way to the top only grows and grows.

Having played in the Gloucestershire age-group pathway for a couple of seasons and then for the South West of England side, I had missed out on making it into the full England age-group sides, which was a crushing disappointment for me.

It didn't stop me progressing in the teams I did play for and by the following summer I was starting to play second-team cricket for Gloucestershire and had begun my professional journey.

In 1981 I made my first-class debut for the county, and I also made my first England appearances too, for the Young Cricketers in two 'Test' matches against India. They would be called the Under-19s now and it was a great thrill to be able to pull on a blazer and a sweater with the England emblem.

As things progressed I found myself getting closer and closer to that dream, and by 1985 I thought that I would make the breakthrough. I had enjoyed a terrific season alongside Courtney Walsh and throughout that summer I was being talked up as England's next fast bowler. I thought I'd be ready for it because I felt so strong and fearless. I could do anything.

When the day came around for the squad to be named, I was feeling pretty confident. England had just beaten Australia 3-1 to win the Ashes, but it wasn't a particularly high-quality series. The real contest in the game came against the West Indies, who were the kings of the world.

I knew just how good they were because Courtney was still finding it tough to nail down a regular spot in the side. But we both spoke about how good it would be if we could play against each other in a Test match. That was the dream, just as it was to play alongside Jack Russell as well. Thankfully they both happened in my career, but it wasn't going to be in the 1985/86 winter.

The squad was named and there was no place for young tearaway David Lawrence. Instead they went with the medium-pace offerings of Greg Thomas and Les Taylor! What are you going to do in the Caribbean with Les Taylor? I can tell you. It is the square root of sod all. He didn't even get a game in the five-Test series, just playing in the odd tour match as England were soundly thrashed 5-0. I don't have any gripe with Les, who was as solid a county pro as you will find, but at international level against that Windies side in the Caribbean, you've got to have something to throw back at the opposition, and Greg Thomas and Les Taylor weren't it.

Peter May was the chairman of selectors and I'm just not sure what the criteria for selection was at times. I was absolutely fuming at that decision and once that subsided I was just gutted that I wasn't going to get a chance in the Caribbean. Instead I was sent to fast-bowling purgatory. Also known as Sri Lanka.

At the end of that season, my performances earned me the award for the Young Player of the Year, as chosen by the Cricket Writers' Club. It is the oldest individual award of its type in the game and is voted on each year by over 400 members who spend their time watching more cricket than anyone else in the land. So if you win, you know you have achieved something special.

What made that award extra special was the fact that it was presented to me by the patron of Gloucestershire Cricket Club the following spring... the Princess of Wales. It was a memorable day as Princess Diana visited the club and had a tour of all the facilities, including watching us have a net. I was only jogging in off a few paces but she still thought I bowled extremely fast! We spoke on several occasions throughout her visit and it was a day I have never forgotten. Naturally I was shocked at the news of her sudden death in 1997 and thought back many times to that day she spent with us at Gloucestershire.

As a result of her patronage three people from the club were invited to her funeral at Westminster Abbey and I was one of those asked to attend. Jack Russell and Andy Stovold were the other two and we went to pay our respects on behalf of the club.

I had been to a few grand occasions over the years but nothing compared to this. Everywhere you looked you saw someone you recognised from the TV and from all sorts of different industries. As we filed into the Abbey, I looked around and thought to myself, 'If I'd been told as a young lad in Gloucester that I would end up at the biggest royal event in the world and be listening to Elton John sing his personal tribute to the Princess, I would never have believed it'.

We could see the coffin being brought in by the young lads in full military dress and they were struggling. It was a hot day and the coffin was lead-lined, so it was extremely heavy. But they did a great job.

The only frustration was the fact we were sat directly behind a couple of Americans. One was Dr Henry Kissinger, a former US secretary of state and brilliant political thinker, the other was Ruby Wax, a comedian, actress and writer who often appeared on television throughout the 1980s and 90s. She would not shut up!

I don't think I've ever heard someone talk as incessantly as she did that day. At one point Jack leaned forward and gently motioned for her to be quiet. She smiled and agreed to do just that, and promptly started talking again.

When I spoke with Diana back in 1986 she did ask me about playing for England and whether it might happen soon. I told her I hoped so, and that if I played at Lord's then I might meet her mother-in-law too.

She had a chuckle at that, which I dined out on for a little while. She was just a very warm and gentle person who had time for everyone. I could imagine that she had to go to so many of these events and could find them quite dull, but she didn't show it at all.

She spoke to all my family who were there and everyone enjoyed meeting her. After the official part of the day was over, we spoke again, and I suggested that she might be able to have a gin and tonic now her duties were complete. She smiled and agreed that would be an ideal drink for her. She was very elegant, very demure, and with beautiful eyes that actually looked at you when you were talking to her, rather than over your shoulder.

It was another two years before I got my first call-up to the England side, and the news travelled to me very slow indeed. Communication is so much easier now than it was back in the 80s. Everyone has a mobile phone and is contactable instantly so when a new player is picked for England it is straightforward to let them know.

And times have changed emotionally too, in that the ECB always make sure that any new player is told by a phone call from the selectors before anyone else is informed.

That is the right way to do it, I think. But when the team was picked in the 80s, you might not get a call until the news had already been released and your quickest way to find out would often be to listen to the names being read out on the radio or maybe reading it on Teletext.

You would also then receive an official letter from the chairman of selectors, which I don't think they send any more, 'inviting' you to play for England. In 1988 the Windies were touring again, so Courtney was unavailable to Gloucestershire until late in the season. We had Aussie bowler Terry Alderman join us in his place.

I'd been injured at the back end of the 1987 season so was keen to have a decent start to the season, but I took a little bit of time to hit my straps. Once I did I really enjoyed my bowling and started catching the eye again.

There were two stand-out performances that really helped my case, first against Essex in Ilford, where I took 7-85 in their second innings, against a team that included Aussie great Allan Border.

And then a month later I took my career-best figures of 7-47 against Surrey at the Cheltenham Festival, which got people wondering whether I might make the England team for the final Test of the series against West Indies at The Oval.

England were in disarray that summer, beaten from pillar to post and using four captains in the process. By the time that final Test came around, Graham Gooch was in charge and so there was no great surprise that the team had an Essex vibe, with seam bowlers Neil Foster and Derek Pringle joined by left-arm spinner John Childs.

With the series lost 4-0, there was one more assignment for England that summer in the shape of a one-off Test against Sri Lanka at Lord's.

I hadn't been given any indication that I might be selected, so wasn't paying any attention to the announcement, especially as my focus was on a friend's wedding. It was a Friday afternoon and I hadn't told anyone where I was going because it was a secret wedding. The groom didn't want anybody to know about it bar the witnesses, of which I was one.

We went to Wandsworth registry office in London to conduct the formalities and once that was done we went to Marco Pierre White's restaurant Harvey's to celebrate.

As we were crossing the road to the restaurant someone saw me and shouted, 'Good luck next week!' Which utterly confused me. I genuinely thought it was a case of mistaken identity and so I took no notice of it and carried on with my night. I had the weekend off so enjoyed myself down in London and returned to Bristol on the Sunday morning. Almost as soon as I got into the house the phone went and it was my mum.

'Hello David. Don't you know you've been picked for England?!' was her opening line.

'I don't think so Mum, it must be speculation, I haven't heard anything about that.'

She sounded very sure that I had been, so I promised I would check it out and let her know if it was true or not.

Once I put the phone down, I noticed that I had a few messages on the answering machine, and each one was the same: 'Hello Syd, just calling you from the club, can you give us a call please.' I called the club and got the news confirmed. I had been picked for England and was going to make my Test debut!

I was thrilled and excited and wanted to let everybody know. Starting with my mum I made calls to my family and close friends, and apart from one or two, everybody already knew. I didn't care. I was going to become an England cricketer and that was that.

A couple of days later I got a white card, a little bigger than a postcard, which invited me to play for England.

It was a hugely proud moment, particularly for my parents who had travelled over to the UK and made so many sacrifices. Now their son was going to represent the country where they had set up their home and raised a family. That was pretty special for them.

Another great aspect about the call-up was that I was going to make my Test debut alongside one of my best friends in the game, Jack Russell.

The dream we had spoken about for years was going to come true and all week we chatted about making sure we got ct Russell b Lawrence into the England scorebook. No-one could take that away from us.

We were both so excited about making our debut and we tried as much as possible to soak it all in. There was a moment for me that was one of the happiest in my career.

Back in the late 70s, I had gone on a school trip to London with a teacher called Mr O'Neill and he took us to Lord's when Middlesex were playing. That was the first time I had ever been to the ground and even though it wasn't a shiny as it is now with the various developments, it was still an incredible ground.

I was in my early years of falling in love with the game but I knew that this was a special place and it got me thinking about what it might be like to actually walk out onto that field and play a game there.

I can remember looking up at the pavilion and the home-team balcony and seeing Barbadian bowler Wayne Daniel sitting there looking magnificent. He had been one of the West Indies bowlers that I had been so impressed by at The Oval just a few years earlier and I thought to myself, 'My goodness, one day I would love to be up there where he is sat. That would be a dream come true.'

So here I was just over 10 years' later and I went out sat down in the very same spot where Wayne had been sitting and looked out across the ground. I just took a moment and thought, 'I wonder if there are any kids out there in the crowd, looking up at me and thinking the same thing I did, and hoping that one day they might be up here.'

I'd like to think that my presence in the England team might have inspired others to achieve their dreams as I had done.

My focus was soon back on the match in hand and Jack and I were happy that England chose to field first so that we could get into the game straightaway. I opened the bowling with Neil Foster, who chose to start from the Nursery End, so I began from the Pavilion End. As I turned at the top of my mark, my stomach was doing cartwheels.

I just wanted to get off to a good start. An early wicket would have been ideal, to settle the nerves and get me up and running. But I also knew from my very first experience as a first-class cricketer that nothing comes easily in sport, and you're not owed anything.

So I couldn't have been happier when, in just my second over, I teased an edge out of their opening batter Amal Silva that headed straight for Jack's gloves.

It wasn't an obvious edge though, more of a faint deflection, but I knew he had hit it, so I started to celebrate. My very first Test wicket was going to be caught by my old mate who had never dropped a catch off me... until now. As it carried to him there was a muted appeal in the slips, but the ball simply flew through his gloves and hit the turf. I couldn't believe it. Jack Russell, one of the finest glovemen to ever play the game, and my mate, dropped my first chance as a Test bowler. I had to smile, because that is the game.

Jack apologised, but he didn't have to. No-one had taken more catches to help get me into this position, it was just one of those things. We still talk and laugh about it to this day.

I asked him about it knowing I'd make mention of it in this book and he said: 'That was our dream, and we talked about it all the time. And it was a miracle that we were picked to make our debut in the same game. I just remember the ball going through my hands, which were so far apart. In my defence, and with it being at Lord's, it did swing and dip on me. After all those years and all those conversations, when it came to the moment, I let Syd down. We then didn't play together for another three years and I wondered whether we would ever get the chance to combine for England as we had done for Gloucestershire, and thankfully we got it.'

Jack and I go way back, not just as Gloucestershire teammates, but as junior cricketers playing for our clubs on the local scene. Jack was a bit of a superstar for Stroud Cricket Club and was talked about as a potential professional when he was just a lad.

I emerged a little later than he did, but we enjoyed some great battles for our respective clubs and started to get to know each other a bit as opponents before we started playing on the same team.

The contests between us were very competitive and neither one of us would back down. The determined and high-quality cricketer that you saw play for England was the same as the young lad I used to play against. He wouldn't give up his wicket easily to anyone, and if there was someone like me causing havoc, then that would just make him more determined.

He would frustrate the hell out of me, and I must admit that once he became a regular teammate of mine at Gloucestershire I was delighted to have him on my side and watch him annoy the opposition.

Our relationship as bowler and keeper was a good one and we understood that we both needed each other in order to succeed and help our teams do well. It wasn't as many as we both would have liked, but to have played four out of my five Tests alongside Jack was really special. I was able to come into the side and focus on the job in hand without too much of a circus around me. There was a bit of media to do, although not quite the same level as there is now, and during that I spoke about the pride I had at being the first UK-born Black cricketer to play for England.

Up until that point Black players who had represented England such as Roland Butcher, Norman Cowans and Gladstone Small, had all been born overseas in various Caribbean territories before moving to the UK as youngsters.

I just happened to be the first to make it to the national side having been born here, even though my family and household was very much a Jamaican one.

With time I have taken more and more pride in being the first, with players such as Mark Butcher, Alex Tudor and Michael Carberry following suit.

However, there has not been the steady flow of young Black talent into the game as we've seen in football. Perhaps the emergence of the ACE (African-Caribbean Engagement) Programme through some brilliant work from Ebony Rainford-Brent will provide more opportunity. We will see. The talent has always been there, but it has often been ignored.

* * *

It felt so special to be making my Test debut at Lord's, a place steeped in cricket history.

I didn't quite get the perfect start with Jack dropping that chance, but I did register my first Test wicket later that day when Duleep Mendis had a bit of a swish at one outside the off stump. He got a thick outside edge and the ball flew away to wide third-man, and my good friend Robin Smith took a good low catch. Aged 24 I had now joined the ranks of Test wicket-takers.

Unfortunately it was the only one I took in the first innings, but I managed to take another two in the second as my first Test match ended in a seven-wicket win. A good start, I thought.

And crucially it was enough to get myself on the tour to India that winter where I felt I could start to show what I was really capable of. This is where I wanted to be and I could see myself getting better and better the more I played alongside and against the best in the game.

But sooner after the squad been announced, trouble started brewing. During the 1980s, apartheid in South Africa was a hot topic and crossed the divide between politics and sport. The regime in South Africa that repressed and oppressed the Black population disgusted many, but there were still plenty of people who chose to look the other way if the money was good enough.

An international sporting boycott was in place and in a sports-mad country like South Africa it was having a real impact on the isolated nation.

Some sportsmen chose to ignore the boycott and either take part in rebel tours to the country or visit it personally, and in the case of several cricketers, play in domestic leagues and do some coaching while they were there. The financial security those trips offered was too tempting for several people to say no to.

Those who had travelled to South Africa independently to play for teams thought they were able to return and play in England without penalty, but those who took part in rebel tours as an 'English XI' knew they would face a three-year ban from international cricket.

What all of those players failed to consider were the wider ramifications. In addition to the captain Graham Gooch, who had led the first rebel tour in 1982, there were seven other players placed on a UN blacklist as a result of playing in South African during apartheid. Kim Barnett, Allan Lamb and Philip Newport had played there the previous winter, while John Emburey, Rob Bailey, Graham Dilley and Tim Robinson were on the list from previous winters.

As a result, all eight players were refused visas by the Indian government, who upheld the UN position, and the tour was placed in jeopardy.

The Test and County Cricket Board could have backed down and picked players who had no connections to South Africa, but instead it ploughed on with the squad that had been picked.

The tour to India appeared it was dead in the water. It looked like we would be heading to New Zealand to play them and Pakistan, but again there was huge opposition to the South African connections and at the 11th hour, with us all gathered at the airport ready to go, it was cancelled.

I felt robbed. Robbed of a tour, robbed of possibly more Test matches. And it still leaves a bitter taste in my mouth. My first

England tour, ripped away from me by something that had little to do with cricket, and I wasn't the only one who missed out.

The South Africa issue was a big one in cricket and I must admit I had a problem with the way a lot of my teammates and people in the game viewed it.

Back then you would go to PCA meetings and people would be there trying to justify why they were going to South Africa. A lot of players would play county cricket in the summer and then swan off to South Africa in the winter, and they would say: 'Don't worry, we are doing our bit over there. We go into the townships and do some coaching.' And that was their justification for going over there and giving an ugly regime their stamp of approval.

I had a lot of conversations about it with Nigel Felton, who was born in Surrey, but his heritage was from South Africa and he would have been referred to as Cape Coloured rather than Black African. Life still wasn't great for them in South Africa. I know Nigel went there after South Africa were readmitted, specifically to play for non-white teams and to try and improve the lot of non-white players. He was a big voice in county cricket at the time, arguing against normalising of sport during apartheid, but people just ignored him. I'm not sure we did enough as a game, we could have been stronger.

We were effectively supporting a regime that was totally wrong. As an association we were saying it was OK for players to go there because they had to find employment during the winter months. But while the phrase 'I've got to earn a living' would be a familiar refrain, precious few people were going to India or Pakistan to earn a living where they might also improve their ability to play spin.

They were going because it was a lovely life, great weather, barbecues, and the money was good, but the political situation was something that was conveniently ignored.

Things came to a head in 1989 when the political system in South Africa was finally breaking and the release of Nelson Mandela was on the horizon. Mike Gatting was gearing up to take another rebel tour over there, which was rightly met with huge anger and protests. The manager for that tour was David Graveney, my captain for a time at Gloucestershire, but he never said a word about what he was up to, which was bitterly disappointing. Maybe he knew that I would have told him how awful I thought it was to try and normalise cricket in a country that wasn't normal. Maybe he didn't want to have that awkward conversation where he would have to justify to his Black teammate why he was happy to travel and entertain a crowd who did not treat Black people like equals.

The practice of apartheid was wrong and he knew it. Everyone knew it. Grav had played for years with me and Courtney Walsh in the Gloucestershire side, and even though I knew there were some who had less liberal views than others, we were a team and we worked towards a common goal every time we walked on the pitch.

For him to not even mention his part in the rebel tour to either Courtney or myself I thought showed a total lack of respect. Because a few days later during the Old Trafford Test, the news broke that he was managing the tour and three of the players in the England side were joining him.

As you can imagine that was the subject everyone was talking about in the Gloucestershire changing room, with our captain Bill Athey also going. I was asked so many times about what I thought about another rebel tour to South Africa and this time under my former captain. I wasn't supportive in any way.

Those who went on the tour were asked about their reasons for going and the answer would often come back that they were going for the good of cricket. I call bullshit on that.

Just say you are going to line your pockets. Be honest. I'd respect you more if you were honest about it.

Also named in the squad were Phil DeFreitas and Roland Butcher, two Black cricketers who had played for England. Butch, in fact was the first, while Daffy had helped England win the Ashes Down Under in 1986/87.

It was clear that they wanted to have some Black players in the squad. It maybe explains why Grav didn't want to bring it up with me and have me chatting to two guys I knew and would tell how I felt.

Both Butch and Daffy pulled out of the trip following the outcry at their involvement and I would think that they were glad they did so considering the protests that met the players in South Africa. It would have been even worse for them.

I would never have gone, although I can understand why some players did. There were plenty of West Indian players who went on rebel tours for whom the opportunity was too lucrative to turn down, but it ruined many of their lives, such was the vitriol against them.

In the end for many of the England rebel tourists their actions didn't cause too many issues. Both Gooch and Gatting played for England again after their bans and in Gooch's case he went on to captain England after leading a rebel tour.

My focus was entirely on playing as much as I could for England and 1989 had been such a write-off for both myself with an Achilles injury and the faltering team that there was no way I'd be ready to face a ban and kill my England dream after one Test. I had more to achieve and I was determined that I would get noticed for the right reasons.

In 1990 I was invited along to an England get-together at Lord's where current and prospective players were all gathered for a spot of training and a lunch.

I thought it was a good thing and it made me feel like I was starting to become a part of the environment and that another international cap might not be too far away.

That theory was swiftly put to bed when one of the selectors, Ted Dexter, strolled over and greeted me with the words: 'How are you doing Gladstone?!'For those not familiar with Gladstone Small, he was a quick bowler who played for Warwickshire and went on to play for England many times, but owing to the genetic condition Klippel-Feil syndrome, where there is a fusing of the vertebrae in the neck, Gladstone was one of the most recognisable sportsmen in the country. For Ted to mistake me for someone else made me wonder whether the selectors had any real clue who I was at all.

CHAPTER ELEVEN

Recall

Going into the 1989 summer I was full of optimism that I could add to my solitary Test cap, but I missed out royally. While England were beaten handsomely 4-0 by Australia, I was struggling with an Achilles injury all season which meant I never really got going.

By the time the squad to West Indies was named I had slipped down the pecking order behind Phil DeFreitas, Gladstone Small, Devon Malcolm, Ricky Ellcock and Angus Fraser.

I didn't even make it into the England A squad to tour Zimbabwe and Kenya in February/March. However, just before that tour was due to depart, Ricky suffered a back injury and sadly for him it was the beginning of the end of his career. He never managed to take the field as an England player. He had real pace too, and I sometimes wonder what it might have looked like if he, Devon and myself were all fit and firing at the same time.

With Ricky sidelined they called up Chris Lewis from the 'A' tour to replace him and so I got my chance as a replacement for Chris.

I was still searching for full match fitness on that trip and played only four of the 13 games, but I enjoyed the tour hugely and was proud as anything to pull on the England shirt overseas.

The 1990 summer that followed seemed to happen around me rather than me doing anything to impact it in a meaningful way. I played more cricket than the year before and my body was holding up alright, but I just couldn't seem to find the rhythm I was looking for.

England were doing well against New Zealand and India and I wasn't realistically in the frame for selection at any stage. It wasn't until the start of the following season that things started to click for me. I began the summer in great form, taking plenty of wickets, and by the time the international matches came round I was being talked about as an option to face West Indies. I was finally picked again for England three years after my previous outing, but this time it was in a one-day international. It was the third of three and England were amazingly already 2-0 up.

I was so proud to be back in an England shirt and this time I had the chance to take on my old friend Courtney Walsh.

Nothing says friendship more than taking your mate's wicket and reminding them of it for days and months afterwards. The scorebook will always read Walsh lbw Lawrence 0, and while neither of us ever won any plaudits for our batting, that wicket is still one of my proudest.

I took 4-67 and kept my name firmly in the conversation for the five-match Test series that was about to get underway. They also happened to be the best bowling figures by any player in ODI history who only played a single match. There is no question I would have given up that record to have played a few more. As good as it was playing in an ODI against the Windies, my heart was set on being involved in the Test series, which was where you knew you would be tested.

They were still the best team in the world at that stage before the Australians had really emerged as the next powerhouse. And they still had my biggest hero in the side in Viv Richards. I missed out in the first two Tests at Headingley and Lord's as Steve Watkin was given his debut, but I was recalled for the third at Trent Bridge and was straining at the leash to get stuck in.

I picked up three wickets in the match but was pretty expensive and the Windies batters, used to high pace back in the Caribbean, picked me off a lot more straightforwardly than I had hoped they would.

There were moments when I gave them the hurry up, but they were few and far between, and in the end they outclassed us to win by seven wickets and draw level at 1-1 with two games left to play.

I was left out of the next game at Edgbaston where the Windies took a 2-1 lead with just The Oval to come.

Such was the haphazard nature of selection you could find yourself cut adrift after just one game, but you could also find yourself back in favour out of nowhere. Players were picked, dropped, recalled and released at the whim of the selectors and you were expected to just get on with it. No wonder our results were all over the place during the 80s and 90s.

Thankfully I was back in business as one of five changes for the last game at The Oval, including a recall for Phil Tufnell who would become one of my great mates. This was what I had started playing cricket for. The chance to face down the great West Indies team at The Oval – the ground where I had first fallen in love with the game through watching the Clive Lloyd team in 1976.

The ground had changed a fair bit in the intervening 15 years, but I could still remember where I had sat and where my dad and his friends had been gathered.

Once the game got underway I was fully focused on the job in hand. We were trying to level the series, but all eyes were on Viv Richards who had announced it would be his last Test match. I still had the words he told me as a young player at Gloucestershire rattling around in my head and was so pleased that I was going to be sharing the field with him for the final time. Once I had the ball in my hand though there was no room for sentimentality. The best way to show respect for this great player was to go toe-to-toe with him and show him how good you were, so that is what I tried to do.

Robin Smith scored a brilliant hundred in the first innings to help get us to 419 all out and then after I removed Phil Simmons to take the first wicket in their reply, Tuffers ran through their side to take 6-25, reminding everyone how good he could be and giving us the chance to enforce the follow-on.

In the second innings I enjoyed my best time as an England bowler with two landmarks I am hugely proud of.

The first of these came midway through the innings. I had already got rid of Desmond Haynes, but Viv was batting very nicely and had moved past his half-century.

The pitch was a little two-paced and sometimes the ball wasn't quite coming on to the bat as expected, but Viv wasn't having too much trouble, until one delivery.

I could tell you how I positioned my field just right for the ball, which was always going to be angled in at the pads, sticking in the pitch a little bit so that Viv would get his timing wrong and pop a catch up to the waiting fielder. And sometimes when I'm telling this story that's exactly how I describe it. But the footage is on YouTube for the world to see. I turned at the top of my mark and ran in to bowl with my usual gusto and as the ball reached Viv, he had already opened up his stance with the intention of whacking me hard and high back over my head for four or even six.

He had done that before to so many bowlers including myself, but on this rare occasion, with the crowd yearning for him to keep going and sign off his career with another hundred, he didn't connect how he meant to.

The ball flew off the inside half of his bat and went straight to Hugh Morris, standing at mid-wicket. He took the catch and threw it high into the air. We were all ecstatic to have removed the dangerous Viv Richards for the last time. I pumped the air with my fist and you can see a huge grin on my face because I had dismissed one of my heroes and had done something good for my team.

Viv set off towards the dressing rooms with the whole ground rising as one to acclaim one of the greatest to have ever played the game. He gave a wry smile as he walked off and every single member of our team stood and applauded him. He might have hurt us with his batting many times, but there was nothing but respect for him as a player and a captain of one of the finest sports teams in history.

As he climbed the steps, and we started to get ready for the next player, that is when it dawned on me: nobody else would ever take Viv's wicket in a Test match again.

I would always be the last bowler to get him out and that made me proud, because he'd had a hand in getting me there in the first place.

The game carried on and I picked up wicket-keeper Jeffrey Dujon fairly quickly, but Malcolm Marshall and Courtney Walsh both hung around to support Richie Richardson, who made a century. I was a little unlucky with a few edges flying to the boundary, but I managed to draw the innings to a close by removing my good mate Courtney and then Richie became by fifth victim to secure my first Test-match five-wicket haul. I thought it would be the first of many now that I had really shown I belonged at this level.

We went on to win the match by five wickets, chasing down 143.

Both myself and Tuffers were not great watchers and we found ourselves in the physio's room listening to the drama and just hoping the batters did the business. Tuffers was looking for somewhere to take a nap, while I was getting some treatment after bowling. Each time the crowd cheered we weren't sure whether it was for a four or for a wicket, so we had to see how people were reacting in the dressing room to work out whether it was good news or bad. Neither of us wanted to get padded up and go out there, and thankfully we didn't.

The win meant we had drawn a hugely competitive series with the best side in the world 2-2 and we celebrated that evening after enjoying a drink with the Windies guys and showing our appreciation of Viv.

Ian Botham was in our side and he and Viv went way back to their early days in Somerset together and they were really close friends, so it was great to hear Beefy talk about his 'brother Viv' at the end of the match.

About a week later we had another one-off Test against Sri Lanka at Lord's which went very well and resulted in a straightforward win. I picked up four wickets in the match as Phil DeFreitas had a field day in the first innings with 7-70 while Tuffers grabbed 5-94 to seal the game.

I had now played in four Test matches and won three of them. Things were going really well and having missed out on the chance to tour with England in 1989, I was finally going to go on my first full England tour, to New Zealand.

Life off the field was going pretty well too. My wife Gaynor was pregnant with our son that summer so the future was opening up before my very eyes. I was going to become a father and all being well I would be an England regular for the foreseeable future.

We were scheduled to fly to New Zealand straight after Christmas so we celebrated the New Year in Auckland. Graham Gooch was our captain and after the palaver around the tour to India that was called off due to his and others' previous visits to apartheid South Africa, there was no such issue with New Zealand.

There were three Tests scheduled and three ODIs all coming ahead of a World Cup in Australia and New Zealand where England went on to do rather well.

Goochie was a man after my own heart when it came to player fitness and it is no surprise that he continued to churn out the runs for Essex and England into his 40s. I have always loved the gym and being in good physical shape to do what I needed to on the field.

As a fast bowler I always wanted to be able to run in and bowl fast whenever my captain asked me to and that meant in the first over of the day or the last. That was something I prided myself on.

Goochie felt that England's cricketers were not always the fittest and that it could cost them when matches went down to the wire. He was determined that, under his watch, England would be fitter than ever. As a result, he instigated an individually crafted fitness plan for each player and then a training camp for the squad in the run-up to Christmas to make sure that when we turned up to fly to New Zealand we were in good shape and could hit the ground running.

We did a lot of fitness work at Lilleshall where we trained, and then had indoor nets to keep the cricket muscles ticking over. Colin Tomlin was our new fitness coach and he had us doing lots of sprints and flexibility exercises, plus the bleep test that everyone hated, even me.

The indoor nets we had were not in a cricket-specific venue, so the ground was rock hard and we just laid down a felt mat that we used to bat on, but we made do.

I don't know whether bowling on such a hard floor before flying out to New Zealand had any impact on what was to subsequently happen to me, but my teammate Jack Russell thinks so.

My son Buster was born at the start of November and we fell in love immediately and just enjoyed that period together as a family, our first Christmas together as a trio. It was a very special time for us, and even though I had to say goodbye to them earlier than I wanted, I was doing it for us. This was my career, and hopefully it would be a long one in the England side.

We left London a couple of days after Christmas and got into our tour with a few warm-up matches. To begin with I felt pretty good. I was bowling with good pace, and in my second game in Napier I took five wickets. To start things off I had Trevor Franklin caught behind, but he wasn't happy.

He insisted the ball had come off his arm and not his glove. He was taken to the local hospital for an X-ray and later that day he came back and he showed the umpires where the arm had been broken, which proved he shouldn't have been given out.

It had been a year since his last Test and he was supposed to open the batting for New Zealand in the Test series against us. He wasn't selected for New Zealand again. Nothing is guaranteed in sport or in life, as I was about to find out.

In the second innings I picked up a rib injury that kept me out of action for a few weeks.

I worked hard to get myself fit and and available once more, but I missed the first two Tests and it wasn't until the third that I was able to play.

CHAPTER TWELVE

New Zealand, New Knee

Talking for any length is really hard now. It seriously tires me out and I just can't get the volume in my voice. I am almost at a whisper and it is hard for anyone apart from Gaynor and Alistair Baker to understand me. It means that I have to repeat myself which is doubly frustrating.

Bit by bit I'm being stripped back. I'm disappearing before my own eyes in more ways than one.

I knew very early on in this process that my voice would diminish, and I knew that would be a cruel blow because my voice has been a big part of who I am. I had the sound to match the body and it was distinctive and recognisable.

* * *

Back in New Zealand I had been having a good time, despite the rib injury. I had been getting my training in during the day and I had found a few guys who were happy to explore the nightlife later on.

One of them was Tuffers, who was a funny bloke and didn't take life too seriously. He was a very talented bowler and he picked up a stack of wickets the previous summer against the Windies.

We got on pretty well during that series, and then our friendship developed a little bit in New Zealand, but the reason we actually ended up becoming really firm friends was because of my booming voice.

Several years later when we had both retired from playing, Tuffers found himself in Southern Spain on holiday and one morning he nipped out for some supplies from the local mini-market. For Tuffers that meant some snacks, a bottle of water and a load of cigarettes. While he was having a nose around, he heard something that piqued his interest. It was a voice he thought he knew. He listened a moment longer, and then it was unmistakable. 'Oi Oi! Hello Syd! I thought I knew that voice!' We greeted each other like long lost brothers and had a nice little catch-up. That could have been that but instead I invited him out for a meal that evening and boy am I glad I did. He and his wife Dawn joined us at El Oceano and we had a cracking night. Gaynor and Dawn hit it off and we all just had so much fun. We then went out again for another night before the holiday was over.

That was the re-start of a beautiful friendship and we have stayed in touch as families ever since. We have been round to each other's houses so many times and Tuffers is one of my very best friends. He's been a huge source of support. Just as he was back in New Zealand in 1992.

Back then I had been getting over that rib injury which had cleared up well enough that I was declared fit to play, and immediately they told me that I would be involved in the next match in Wellington. That was a good confidence booster and told me how highly they thought of me.

I got myself ready, but I didn't really feel that great. My speed was down and my left knee was giving me a bit of concern, but nothing beyond what you would call a niggle.

We bat first and I spend the first day resting up. Days two and three are a nightmare as New Zealand bat and bat. They take 192 overs to score their 432-9 and I am fairly done in by the end of it. I send down 27 overs but thankfully we have the spin of Tuffers and Graeme Hick to do most of the work. We are in the field for almost two entire days and even just standing and fielding takes its toll.

The game is heading towards a draw and on the last day we decide to bowl a few more overs in the second innings. That morning I spoke to our physio Laurie Brown and told him that something wasn't quite right with my knee and asked him to take a look at it. I asked him what he thought the problem was.

He said: 'Syd, what you've got is 'housemaid's knee'.

I replied: 'Sorry, but what the fuck is housemaid's knee?!'

'It is when you spend a long time on your knees like a housemaid or a cleaner and you get the resulting pain from that,' he explained.

'But I don't spend any time on my knees, Laurie! I haven't got a job where I'm on my knees. What am I supposed to do with this diagnosis?!'

Anyway, I'm none the wiser as to what really is going on and I just go out there and get on with it. I start bowling and it really isn't coming out that well, so after a couple of overs Jack Russell comes over to me. He has been keeping to me for about 15 years and he knows when I'm not hitting the gloves hard.

He asks: 'Are you ok? You're not quite hitting the gloves the way you normally do.'

Now, this would be the time to admit that I'm not feeling great and that my knee is really struggling. Maybe even tell the captain that I need to go off rather than keep bowling. I don't do that.

I think, 'I'll show him how hard I can hit the gloves.'

I turn at the top of my mark and run in and as I land in my delivery stride, my knee just explodes and the crack can be heard in every part of the ground.

Never mind the fact that the Basin Reserve is in the middle of a giant roundabout. My knee can be heard above all the cars and lorries, and it is swiftly followed by the screams of anguish and pain that I can't keep in. It is the most painful thing I have ever felt, and I'm sobbing.

There is no amount of toughness, strength or endurance that can prepare you for a moment when your kneecap breaks and splits in two, with one half staying put and the other half in your thigh. Sorry to be so graphic, but it was excruciating.

It felt like a sniper had shot me in the knee and the whole thing was just ripped apart.

The players on the field were in shock and tried to help me as the medics and physios ran out and arranged for me to be carried off the field. Lots of players helped carry me off, Ian Botham playing in his 100th Test, Derek Pringle, Alec Stewart, and Graeme Hick all helped, and Jack Russell was there too by my side as I came off. I didn't realise until a while later that Jack and Micky Stewart, our manager, had got into an argument with a cameraman who had been filming me coming off.

It was an instinctive human reaction from them to try and protect me and give me some privacy at what was such an awful time.

Their anger at the cameraman caused as much of a stir as the injury itself, which was plastered across the papers the next day. I will always be grateful for their desire to look out for me. I was told that Jack even chased the cameraman up the stairs in the stands as he continued to try and film it. That's what friends are for, and I love Jack for that.

When the players came back onto the field without me, Beefy apparently told the cameraman that he would stick the camera up his backside if he got hold of him.

I only shared a dressing room with Beefy a few times, but I have been in his company on a few occasions over the years and I have no doubt he would have done exactly that. There was a small physio room in the pavilion at the Basin, but it was too small for me to be stretchered into, so they actually took me into the dining room where there was more space and they could lay me out flat on the table. They gave me oxygen and painkillers and started making arrangements for me to go to hospital straight away.

The adrenaline had properly kicked in and things were a bit of a blur, but Jack often reminds me that at this point I actually tried to insist that I could carry on, that I could get back onto the field despite having one half of my kneecap up in my thigh. It was a horrible-looking sight and teammates have told me it remains the most stomach-turning thing they have seen on a sports field.

It was just so visceral, and even though you know that there is always a chance of injury when you go out to play, nobody wants to be reminded just how fragile they are.

I didn't think of myself in that way at all, which is why I was so keen to carry on and prove how tough I was and how much playing for England meant to me.

The pain had subsided thanks to the adrenaline coursing through my body. And rather foolishly I took it to mean that the injury couldn't have been as bad as first feared.

I thought that if I could get back out there and test it out, I could somehow keep going. I really didn't want to leave the field let alone leave the ground for the hospital. So I tried to get up and was immediately pushed back down by Laurie Brown who said I wouldn't be going anywhere.

Well, that seemed like a challenge I had to respond to, so I tried to get up again and was again restrained by Laurie, but I was considerably bigger and stronger than him so he wasn't winning that battle.

At which point a couple of teammates came over to help but I ended up wrestling with them too. I was like a man possessed and the next thing I knew I had pushed Derek Pringle with such force that he collapsed into the chairs nearby.

It was at this point that Laurie said to them, 'Right, leave him be. He will try and stand up and then collapse back in a heap and maybe that will get the message through.'

I got up, the pain was excruciating, and I fell over immediately. I guess Laurie was right about that one.

When I got to the hospital they let me call my partner. I completely forgot about the time difference, but as my son was only three months old she was up anyway. But this wasn't the news she wanted to hear.

I told her: 'You're going to see some pictures on the news today and it doesn't look great. I've had an injury in the game and I'm already at the hospital, but I wanted to tell you before you heard it anywhere else. The good news is that I will be ok, and I'm just going into surgery. Don't worry, it will be alright.'

The surgeons did a fantastic job under the circumstances. They said the patella must have had a hairline fracture in it, which could have occurred through wear and tear. The amount of weight and pressure I was putting through my legs was quite something. I was a powerfully built fast bowler and as a result I had various weak spots throughout my body where they bore the brunt of my work and the kneecap was one of them.

The quad muscle in my left leg had contracted and such was the power and the force of the contraction, it just split the patella in two along the weakness.

The surgeons brought the two halves back together and screwed the kneecap in place with the aim of getting the bone to fuse back together.

A couple of days after the surgery, the boys took it in turns to come and visit me in the hospital where I would be staying for a couple of weeks.

They tried their best to cheer me up, but the recurring theme was just how loud the crack was when I fell to the ground. None of them had ever heard or seen anything like it. Imagine what it felt like to actually experience it. I put on a brave face and talked positively about my return to the side in due course, but we all knew that it wasn't going to be as easy as that. If someone suffered the same injury now, they would have a half-decent chance of getting back to an exceptionally high level, but the odds were completely stacked against you back then.

Even though I didn't admit it to anybody, I lay in the hospital hour after hour wondering what my future held. I spoke to my wife most days and could hear Buster, which cheered me up and had me looking forward to the flight home. But it also made me think about the long road ahead and how I would get myself back on the field.

I had to spend two weeks in hospital in Wellington before I was able to fly and begin that process of rehabilitation and face up to a future that had seemed so full of promise just a few short weeks ago.

Thankfully I had the company of Jack and a couple of others who were heading home after the Test series and who weren't staying on for the World Cup that followed.

I was even bumped up into first class because of the extra space required for my leg. Jack spent most of the time up there with me and we had a reasonable flight home, but my fear that this was already the end of my England career was well-founded. I never played international cricket again.

CHAPTER THIRTEEN

Rehabilitation

I was determined to come back and be just as good as before if not better. It is a sportsman's mindset. The competitive urge to view everything as a battle to win. This was just another contest to come out on top in. And I was used to winning.

I was back and forth with the doctors in Bristol having various X-rays to see how the knee was healing, and as it got stronger and stronger I was able to get more work done in the gym to strengthen and support the knee.

Before all that though, I simply had to rest up and let the kneecap fuse back together, so I found other ways of occupying myself.

I had a young baby to help look after at home so I got more involved with him which was great, although I do wonder whether Gaynor actually found it easier when she didn't have me under her feet as well.

After a week back home, the World Cup was starting to come into sharp focus for my old teammates who were still Down Under.

The tournament was being shown for the first time on satellite television thanks to a deal with the three-year-old network Sky TV.

They had shown live cricket from the West Indies in 1990 for the first time and just weeks ahead of their first foray into showing Premier League football they had the rights to the Cricket World Cup, something they have continued to hold onto until this day.

I got a call from Sky's head of sport asking whether I would join their studio team in the UK as a pundit.

My injury had been front-page news in the national press thanks to the dramatic nature of how it happened, and the fact that there had been some really good and clear photos of me in agony.

Naturally you would prefer for that not to be the case, but it happened in a very public place in a very public way, so you have to accept that people are going to want to see it.

This was where the issue with the cameraman came to a head. He was trying to do his job in a public place, but my teammates were trying to give me a bit of privacy during a traumatic moment. I can see both sides. The reality is that the story probably gained more noise and notoriety thanks to the row over the cameraman than it otherwise would have got.

The front-page coverage enhanced the story and made me someone that people were more interested in, and several opportunities in my life have come about as a result of the public nature of what happened.

Cameras are everywhere now so there isn't really anything of note that doesn't get filmed, and we've become a little blasé about what we see on the internet. When I crumpled in a heap on the field, that was a shocking moment that people wouldn't have seen very often at all, so it made me newsworthy in a way that it probably wouldn't do now. I don't know whether that is a good thing or not. More and more people are getting their 15 minutes of fame these days, but it probably dies away more quickly than ever before.

My misfortune on the field led to an opportunity to do some media work off it, and I took it. I mean, the chance to watch and talk about cricket and air my views on national TV? Where do I sign? This was right up my street.

I was anything but a shrinking violet, I enjoyed the cameras and the lights and the attention that came with being on TV and thought I could do a good job. And it was great fun. If I couldn't be there in person as a part of the squad, then this was the next best thing. I felt very comfortable in front of the camera and thought I looked pretty good too, although I had to carry a cane with me to help me get around as the knee was still sore.

The media world is one that I enjoyed getting a taste of, and there were a few more opportunities to come that I enjoyed, but whether it could be a career for me outside of, or instead of, cricket I wasn't sure.

During the tournament I was asked to appear on a Channel 4 magazine-type programme called *The Word*, which was hosted by a Mancunian called Terry Christian. It was a slightly chaotic show aimed at a young audience and it specialised in causing outrage. It was a mix of celebrity guests and everyday people doing bizarre things, with live music. I thought it might be fun and it would be a trendy show to be on. The only problem was that I was on with a rather odd chap called John Lydon aka Johnny Rotten, the former lead singer of the Sex Pistols. They were a big deal during the punk era of the 1970s, but that wasn't a vibe or groove that I was into at all. I preferred reggae and Northern Soul, and apart from a few tunes by The Clash it wasn't for me.

But I've always liked interesting people, regardless of their background or anything else. My philosophy has always been that people can come together and have a good time no matter how different they are, and I was curious to know what Lydon was like. He was a dick.

I don't know whether it was just the way he was, or if he was playing up to a persona, or whether he had taken something, or had a skinful to drink, but he was just an idiot on the programme. He was looking to wind people up either in the audience or the presenter or me sat on the sofa next to him.

At one stage during his ramblings he called me a 'sheep-shagger' on live TV! As you can imagine I didn't take to that too kindly and told him I'd throw him out of the nearest window.

'Ooh is that a threat?!' He mocked.

'No, but if you find out the time of the next bus, I'll make sure you're under it,' came my reply. I was joking of course, but I can remember thinking, 'I actually want to knock this guy out to shut him up'.

He completely dominated the conversation and at the end of the show Terry turned to me to thank me for coming on but was upset that we hadn't had a chance to talk about my love of Northern Soul and my visits to Wigan Casino.

Earlier on in the conversation, before Lydon turned up, he did ask me about where I came from and suggested that I was from the posh part of Bristol and had a bit of a posh accent.

Perhaps subconsciously I had tried to ditch the Gloucester tones and make myself sound a bit more refined on TV. He asked me whether it was a requirement to be posh to play cricket and I immediately rejected that notion, but I wonder whether he had simply tapped into something that was already on its way. There has always been a class divide in cricket, between the gentlemen and the players, the professionals and the amateurs, the north and the south, and to some extent the batters and the bowlers.

But increasingly the game has become more exclusive and more 'posh' and if Terry Christian were to ask an England player now whether you had to be posh to play professional cricket, the only honest answer would surely be 'not necessarily, but it helps'. He also asked me about my Jamaican parents and whether or not they would support England or West Indies, and then he asked me.

I told him that I was an England fan born and bred, to which he said: 'So Norman Tebbit would let you stay in the country.' I laughed it off, but it stung. Imagine being asked on national TV whether or not you would support the country you were born and raised in knowing that the 'wrong' answer would lead to the suggestion that you shouldn't be allowed to stay. Just think about that for a moment.

Never mind the fact that you've just broken your leg busting a gut to try and win a cricket match for that same country.

Never mind the fact that you were itching to get back into the gym so that you could get fit to try and represent that country once again in the future.

Those rehab sessions throughout the summer of 1992 were tough and lonely at times. Even though I wasn't playing, I enjoyed being around the lads when they were playing at home and I could do some fitness work and then spend a bit of time in the dressing room with them and still feel part of the team.

It wasn't easy being on the sidelines though, because even though the knee was getting stronger, I had no idea whether I'd still be able to bowl well enough to be able to continue my career. It was like a dark cloud hanging over me full of uncertainty.

At least I had the good news that I was to be awarded a benefit for the 1993 season where I could arrange a host of events and fundraising activities that could work alongside my return to cricket following a year out of the game.

I had followed the instructions of the doctors and the physios to the letter and I had various scans of the knee as it started to get stronger and stronger with a view to me returning to play at the start of the 1993 summer.

It was almost a year to the day after suffering the injury when I was in the gym working out and feeling pretty confident about getting myself ready to play at a high level when I did a leg extension on one of the weight machines and... crack! The kneecap snapped again and I was back to square one.

The mind is a funny thing though, and even though I heard the noise, I refused to believe it.

I sat there on the machine, and the adrenaline kicked in so powerfully I just told myself, 'That didn't happen'. I simply shut it out of my mind and ignored it.

I don't know how I did this, but I carried on training. I finished my reps and then walked around and then did some more training on another machine.

Once I'd finished my session, I got into the car to go home and as I put my foot on the clutch to set off, I couldn't feel anything.

It took about 15 minutes for me to actually realise that my kneecap had broken again and it was starting to hurt.

I took myself to the hospital and arrangements were made for another operation to patch it up and see if the bone would actually heal properly this time.

I called my partner and gave her the bad news. And with our little boy now just over a year old, the future started to look a little more bleak.

I'm generally a positive guy and look for the best in any situation, but having just broken my kneecap for the second time in a year, and facing another year out of the game, I was starting to think that maybe I had already come to the end of my cricketing road.

I had stayed optimistic about a comeback after the first injury, because things had been going so well and I was finally starting to cement my place in the England team.

I was still under 30 and felt like my body was fit and strong enough to come back from anything, but this second injury in the same place obviously suggested I would have a weakness here for the long term.

How could I do the hard physical work required of a fast bowler if there was always going to be a danger that my left knee might not be up to it? I had a long road ahead of me to see which way things went, but I can't say that I felt overly optimistic about my chances.

Still, if I was going to retire it would be on my terms and not without giving myself a genuine go at coming back, and that was the thought that grew and grew in my head. I was also not going to walk away from the game at the start of my Benefit summer. I wanted the fans and the supporters who were turning up for my events to know that I was still a Gloucestershire and England cricketer.

The whole point of a Benefit is for the supporters to show their appreciation for your efforts and to reward you for the loyalty and longevity that you have shown.

And even though I had put in over a decade of service to the club, I didn't want to be attending dinners and matches and receiving the profits knowing that I was walking away from the club and the supporters.

I wanted to give it one more shot to see if I might pull on the Gloucestershire shirt again and maybe in my wildest dreams get back to the very pinnacle and play for England again.

So that is what I set about doing, back in the gym – steering clear of leg extensions – doing my stretching and strengthening work, plus lots of cycling which was very gentle on the knee.

The second break was not quite as severe as the first injury which meant that I was able to make progress a little more quickly than the first time around, but I still spent more time than I wanted to on my own and in the gym rather than on the cricket field.

As 1993 took shape I was enjoying the various events for my Benefit from a race day at Cheltenham to a tenpin bowling challenge, to dinners and cricket matches and even a boxing night at the Café Royal.

But above all, my knee was responding well to the physio and rehab work I was doing, so much so that in the David Lawrence XI v Rest of the World XI match that took place at Cheltenham College in the August, I was actually able to take the field and bowl.

Yes, just over six months after breaking my kneecap, I could bowl. The run was more of a jog, and the pace of the bowling was very medium indeed, but it was a really important day for me to show that I could at least think about bowling properly again and that I might still have a future in the game.

For the rest of the summer, I spent more time outside and steadily increased my loads around bowling, although I remained a way off full tilt come the end of the season.

I knew that I wanted to see for myself whether or not I could make a realistic go of things the following summer and I thought the best way to do that was to go back to Australia for another winter and test out the knee.

I didn't want to go with any fanfare or expectation though, because it might all come crashing down the moment I tried to put my foot to the floor.

I had a few friends over in Australia including Mike Whitney who had played for Gloucestershire back in 1981, the same year I made my county debut, before he went on to make his Test debut later in the summer in the Ashes.

He was a very handy left-arm quick and unlucky not to play more than 12 Tests, although he did play almost 50 ODIs and featured in the 1992 World Cup.

He and I remained in touch over the years and he had mentioned in the past about possibly going over and playing a season with his club Randwick. I gave him a call to see whether there might be a chance for me to come over and play a bit of cricket in their second team and just see where I was with my knee. I didn't want any expectation or pressure to perform as the overseas player, I just needed somewhere to get some cricket away from the spotlight.

Mike was great and helped me sort everything out so that I could go and play in their seconds. I knew it would be a half-decent standard of cricket, but one where I thought that I could find my feet and test out my fitness in peace and quiet.

If I finished crumpled in a heap then I knew my cricket days were over, but if my knee stood up to bowling again then I was confident I could give the 1994 summer a go.

When I got on the plane to Australia I genuinely had no idea which way it was going to go. There were days when I felt so good and so strong and so confident, but there were just as many where I didn't think I would be able to get out of bed, let alone go and deliver a ball at any great speed.

When I arrived in Sydney it was tipping it down with rain which should have been an omen, but I saw the positive which was that the ball might do a little bit if there was moisture in the pitches.

By the time I came to play a game, the sun was out, the moisture had gone and the pitches were flat. I sent down a few overs and it felt okay, and crucially there was no reaction from the knee. It was good to get a first game under my belt and even though I felt a little sore just from playing and bowling again, it was a good sore. I played a couple of games without much to report, and then in the third match I was bowling with what felt like some reasonable pace.

This kid comes in to bat and he is not even old enough to order a drink, but he has the sort of confidence that suggests he would give it a go and probably get away with it.

I decide to bowl him a bouncer and he takes it on and hooks me out of the park. I thought, 'Ok, you got away with one. Let's see how you deal with this.' This time I come in to bowl with some real purpose and I put some effort into a much sharper bouncer and he rocks back with even more time than before and hooks me out of the park a second time.

The competitive juices are flowing and I don't like being hit in such an easy way, but the knee is sore so I tighten up my line and length and he gets in behind the ball nicely.

Down at fine-leg my knee is not great. I'm wondering whether it is just because things aren't going my way, but actually there is pain even when I'm not moving it which is a huge worry, but I push it to the back of my mind and come back for another over.

This time the same kid is ready and waiting. I'm less confident about going short at him because he seems to like it there. So I bowl what would be called a good length, not too full, but with the arrogance of youth he walks down the pitch and lofts the ball high back over my head for six.

Well, that was the last straw. I'm not proud of it, but I lost my head and knowing that I couldn't go back at him with my pace like I normally would, I dropped my shoulder as he jogged by me and barged him. I immediately regretted it because that was not the way to behave. I apologised and to his credit he just laughed it off knowing he had won that battle.

At that moment I know I'm done.

The reality is that I'm not the bowler I was and I can't do the things that I used to be able to do. This is what I came to Australia to find out. And even though I didn't like what it was telling me, I had got my answer. Professional cricket for me was over.

You could say that it was a sudden decision made in the heat of battle with emotions running high and feelings of dejection in my mind.

But it had been coming. Of course it had. From the moment I collapsed in a heap at the Basin Reserve, I knew that my career was going to be cut short.

Through all the visits to hospital, chats with doctors, plans devised by physios, training and recovery work in the gym, gradual returns to bowling, and then repeating it all a second time… of course I knew this day was coming.

I might have tried to deny it and put on a brave face and try my best to come back better than ever. But here in Sydney, thousands of miles from home, I knew I was done.

I phoned my mum and dad and my wife that evening and told them the news, and then I called the club and told them that I was going to retire from the game. The response from the secretary was one of sympathy and disappointment, but there wasn't a huge amount of surprise. Once the news was announced to the wider public, it was the same reaction. Everyone was sympathetic and kind but there wasn't much surprise. If anything people were surprised that it had taken as long as it did for me to get to the decision.

They say when it comes to retirement you know when you know, and I think that is true when you are fit and have had a long career and your body catches up with you over time.

But I'm not sure it is true otherwise.

I didn't want to retire at all, but after two attempts to come back and my body not responding in the way it needed to, I didn't feel I had a choice.

CHAPTER FOURTEEN

Giving It Another Go

What is it about fast bowlers and their egos? Actually, scratch that. What is it about sportspeople and their egos?

It is both a blessing and a curse, because I'm not sure you can make it to the very top without having a decent dollop of ego in your make-up. A confidence and a belief that you are either the very best at what you do or, if not, that you can work hard enough and improve enough to get there.

I suppose there are those athletes who have an incredible gift for whatever sport they play, and when they mix that together with the work ethic then they become untouchable. The likes of Muhammad Ali, Viv Richards, Serena Williams and Brian Lara.

But for the rest of us we make the most of what we have and compete as strongly as possible at the highest level, and it is addictive.

It is why I tried to come back so many times as a cricketer, and why I felt the need to have my knee replacement after so many years just getting on with things.

I don't have too many regrets, but one is certainly my third and final attempted comeback as a professional cricketer for Gloucestershire.

In the summer of 1996, just before I opened my first restaurant and wine bar, I had played a series of charity and social matches that turned my head in a way that I couldn't resist.

I was playing for Mr Getty's team at Wormsley on a high-quality pitch and when I found myself bowling to some half-decent players and causing them a few problems I started to think, maybe, just maybe I can still do this.

I had a year and a half where I was training pretty well and felt fitter than I had done for a while, so I thought, why not give it a go?

The truth was that I still hadn't come to terms with how my career had finished. There was an itch that needed scratching and the only way I would reach it would be by trying to play again. I didn't want to be wondering in 30 years' time whether I should have tried again.

I spoke to the club to see whether they would be interested in taking me back on if I could do a job, and they were keen.

Mark Alleyne was the captain and someone who I got on well with and who rated what I could do for a team. He had come into the side as my career was blossoming in the mid-1980s and he had continued to improve ever since.

He was a hugely talented batter and a very skilful and competitive bowler. But his all-round talents also extended to his leadership in the dressing room that saw him become one of the most successful captains in the English game, especially in white-ball cricket.

He commanded the respect of the Gloucestershire dressing room and he was happy to see me back in whites. I played four Championship matches that summer and the results were mixed. There was the high of a memorable win over Surrey at The Oval where I removed both Alec Stewart and Mark Butcher, two England players at the time, and probably surprised both them and myself with how well the ball came out.

Twice dismissing Butch in particular gave me some real joy as he was caught top-edging a couple of hooks towards the long-leg boundary. It suggested to me that I might be able to get back to somewhere near my best.

The knee held up well in those first couple of games against Hampshire and Surrey, but the body was sore and needed more conditioning to play more matches.

I played some second-team cricket and then got myself back in the side to face Nottinghamshire and Kent towards the back end of the season. It was in these games where I started to question my early summer optimism about what I could do.

I felt a bit like a heavyweight boxer who didn't quite have the same punch of a few years before.

I was slower, I was heavier and I didn't have the snap.

The snap is that bit of magic that all fast bowlers look for which gets the ball down the other end quicker than the batter is expecting. It's a combination of athletic prowess, rhythm and skill that gives you something a little more than the sum of its parts. And when you have that snap as a bowler, you are always in the game. Anything can happen. But I didn't have it any more, and I found out in my last game of the season.

I played against Kent at Canterbury and sent down 15 reasonable overs in the first innings, but didn't take any wickets, and didn't really look like taking wickets. It was the second innings where I realised I was being left behind. I only bowled six overs but was clobbered by David Fulton and Ed Smith for 53 runs and I thought, 'This can't go on'. It was a sobering experience and made me think that this return might just be one attempt too far, but I couldn't let it go. I loved playing cricket so much, and I had been robbed of my best years as a fast bowler by injury, so I didn't want to give it up without a real fight.

That winter I buried myself in my restaurant and in the gym. I was determined to be in the best possible shape I could be for the following season, which would have to go really well for me to continue in the game. I trained hard, I lost some weight, and I was focused on giving it a good go.

I began with a couple of second-team matches in April as I looked to force my way back into the first team. I was called into the office of our new head coach John Bracewell who laid it on the line for me.

'Look Syd, these, are my thoughts,' he said. 'We've got South Africa coming up in a tour match in a few weeks, that could be your farewell match. That could be a good game to say goodbye because I don't really see you as part of our plans going forward.' Immediately I responded with the emotion that was at the surface.

'No, no, no, I don't want to go out like that,' I said. 'I've got myself fit and I think I can do more of a job than that.' Inside I was burning up because I had already had my career taken away from me once before, I wasn't going to let someone else take it away from me again.

I was going to go out on my terms, not on somebody else's.

A couple of days later I arranged a meeting with the club during which I relayed what John had told me and said that if the club didn't want my services then I should be able to play elsewhere. They called John into the meeting to clarify his position and he denied saying any of it. I was surprised and quite upset by that. I knew I wasn't wanted so I asked the club to pay me up to the end of my contract and let me go. Initially they didn't want to do that and it led to an unnecessary legal row between me and the club that meant my Gloucestershire career came to quite a sour end, when it could have been avoided.

Looking back on it now, my ego got the better of me. I shouldn't have been so hasty in turning down the opportunity to play in that tour game.

It should have been my farewell match to all the Gloucestershire supporters and to the club after such a long association. I never got the chance to raise my cap to the fans and leave on a happy note and I accept my part in that. It was me being stubborn. I regret that decision for sure.

Sometimes you do need someone to tell you that you're not quite as good as you think you are. You need some home truths and you have to be able to take them. I didn't listen and in the end I'm the one who was hurt by that.

I think back to the way that I felt about apartheid during the 1980s and having seen a rebel tour organised right under my nose – it was a country that meant more to me than a lot of others.

And when I had the opportunity to play against them in fair competition, with Nelson Mandela released, I missed out because a situation of my own making.

I look back on some of the bad decisions I've made in my life and that is definitely one of them. I really regret not taking the field and playing that game against South Africa and leaving Gloucestershire on good terms, but I had to live with it. I was too emotional and I wasn't thinking clearly enough. It left me in turmoil because the club and the game that had given me so much was now putting me on the scrap heap with an uncertain future ahead of me.

I had already had some dark moments around my injury and trying to come back the first time around. I had done a lot of soul searching before finally getting Boom bar off the ground and thankfully by this time it was starting to make some good money.

But the money didn't make up for what I had lost. My purpose in life had been to be the best cricketer I could be, but here I was without that drive any more and I was lost.

The way things ended with Gloucestershire as a player was hugely frustrating, and that year I wasn't the only one to suffer that way.

Recognition: with the England A squad on tour in Zimbabwe; and alongside my England teammates on the Lord's balcony.

Agony.

Ian Botham and Derek Pringle help carry me off at the Basin Reserve.

Putting in the hard yards with physio Laurie Brown.

About to put a lot of force through my body.

Like flying.

Unable to control my emotions after the T20 Blast win.

Ready for my interview.

Having been out to the Caribbean to watch my good friend Courtney Walsh play in a Test against England at Sabina Park, I was looking forward to rekindling our partnership that had brought the club so close to winning a first County Championship crown back in 1986.

We had talked about it briefly in Jamaica because Courtney had missed the 1997 English season to have a deserved break and was ready to go again.

But after one more match for the Gloucestershire first team against Cambridge University, I was done, and Courtney and I would never cross the boundary as county teammates again.

He went on to have a brilliant year for the club, his testimonial, and again got them so close to the promised land with 118 wickets – an incredible number that pushed them to third in the table.

But once it was over, the expected two-year deal that he had verbally agreed with the club was rescinded that winter over the inaccurate suggestion that he was talking to other counties.

The club had simply decided to go in a different, more cost-effective, direction and put more effort into their white-ball cricket. Hence the decision to sign the Australian all-rounder Ian Harvey.

I spoke with Courtney at the time and I know he wasn't happy about the way things were handled and the fact that his 14-year association with the club was ended with a fax. I didn't agree with the decision either, and it added to my feeling of annoyance with the club at a time when I was drifting away from the game. I thought Courtney deserved better and I certainly didn't think that Harvey was a comparable overseas player. I didn't believe he was in Courtney's league as a cricketer or that his recruitment would result in trophy-winning success for the club.

Of course, you have to be prepared to admit when you're wrong, and this was one of those situations. Harvey turned out to be a gem of a cricketer and the catalyst for a period of dominance for Gloucestershire in white-ball cricket. With Mark as skipper they lifted seven one-day trophies in six years in a glorious spell for the club.

It might not have been a decision I agreed with, but they got it right and it made Gloucestershire a real force in the game – ahead of their time and innovative in a way that every other team followed. Of course I wish I could have experienced that feeling of raising a trophy as a player, but it was my team winning and that was the next best thing.

Over the next few years my life would start to go in a different direction and away from cricket for a variety of reasons.

But I think that the slightly awkward and low-key nature of my departure led me to focus my attentions away from the game.

I did have connections with cricket here and there, but the reality was that almost 20 years after beginning my professional career, the game was moving on without me and I without the game.

CHAPTER FIFTEEN

Getty Address

Throughout this book I have made several references to race simply because it has had such a bearing on my life.

I know there will be some people who won't pay any attention to it and will accuse me of making too much of it and finding issues where there are none. But all I can do is tell you my view and how I have felt and how I have interpreted a variety of situations.

The colour of my skin has had an impact for sure, but it hasn't been the determining factor in my life. I have lived a good life, and a largely enjoyable one, and I'm extremely proud to be a Gloucester boy born and bred, but with a deep love for my Caribbean heritage and family. There have been incidents that I've mentioned where the racism has been obvious and in my face, but there will have been many more that I have been unaware of or would be unable to prove.

When Michael Holding and Ebony Rainford-Brent made their brilliant comments on Sky Sports a few years ago and cricket started to do a deep dive into the inequality in the sport around race, gender and sexuality, it revealed things that surprised some people, but came as confirmation to a lot of others.

The sexism and racism that is insidious in society is the worst of all, because it is so hard to pinpoint, but you know it is there. It might be the reason why you don't get that contract, or you don't get that promotion, or you are not given that responsibility, or you are simply watched a little bit more closely when you walk into a shop. These are the downsides of being perceived as different, but you can't live your life worrying about the worst that can happen, sometimes it is important to appreciate it when things go your way too.

Following my knee injury in 1992 and subsequent attempt to come back, by 1995 I had retired from the game accepting that the gig was up and was actively looking at what else I might do with my life. I always had a love of going out and enjoying myself, whether it was at Northern Soul all-nighters in Wigan and Blackpool, or the local nightlife in Bristol. I was a social creature and I loved seeing people have a good time. I always thought that I would end up in that area of the hospitality industry when my career as a cricketer was over. Clearly those thoughts had no surfaced sooner than I had expected.

I had been awarded a Benefit year by Gloucestershire for 1993 which was a welcome distraction for me during my recovery and rehabilitation. It meant that I was able to take a much more hands-on role with the Benefit and attend every function from start to finish as there wasn't any cricket for me to play that summer.

With the money I raised from that year, I was seriously considering using it to invest in a bar or a restaurant for the next phase of my life. I knew nothing about the hospitality industry apart from how to enjoy oneself in it, so I had plenty of work to do to get myself up to speed. I bought a book called 'How to Open a Successful Restaurant' and read it from cover to cover, which gave me an idea of the basics and the direction of travel.

But before I got up and running there was a stroke of luck that came my way thanks to my heritage. Over the course of three articles in *Wisden Cricket Monthly* magazine in 1995, Robert Henderson called into question the selection methods for the England team.

Having taken issue with the Ashes tour party he started to question the merit and the loyalty of players who had not been born and raised in England because he found it hard to believe that they would go the extra mile for the national side if they had arrived from elsewhere.

This totally misunderstands the professionalism and pride that every single player puts in when they pull on an England shirt, no matter where you are born. There is a long and proud history of players playing for adopted countries and performing magnificently. Cricket is a unique individual battle within a team framework so when you are running in to bowl or ready to face the next delivery, you have no thoughts about where you are from or where your opponent is from. It is a simple one-on-one battle that you are trying to win each time. To suggest otherwise is wide of the mark.

I do think we have moved past this debate in England, and it is not an accusation that would be levelled today with any credibility. Certainly you won't find people taking this issue up with the World Cup-winning and Dublin-born Eoin Morgan, nor the New Zealand-born Ben Stokes.

But in 1995 it was given plenty of airtime thanks to the question of the 'Tebbit Test' still being at the forefront of some people's minds. This stemmed from a theory put forward by MP Norman Tebbit that immigrants' offspring supporting their parents' homeland such as India, Pakistan or West Indies rather than England was a sign that they weren't fully integrated into UK society. The idea that you could support the team of your family's heritage in cricket but still be utterly loyal and devoted to the UK as a proud British citizen was not something Mr Tebbit could understand. It wasn't his experience so he had difficulty relating to it, or maybe he didn't want to.

In the third of Henderson's articles titled 'Is it in the blood?' he took things too far when he suggested that the desire to succeed was a question of instinct and biology – and something players of West Indian heritage could not have.

He namechecked Phil DeFreitas and Chris Lewis, asking what they had to be proud of by playing for England, and he even went as far as to suggest that '...part of a coloured England-qualified player feels satisfaction at seeing England humiliated because of post-imperial myths of oppression and exploitation'. Understandably it caused quite a furore at the time and the players involved took legal action against the magazine, edited by David Frith.

I spoke to the guys involved and I was just as angry as they were that the commitment of players with foreign (albeit at one-time British citizens through Empire) heritage was being brought into question. I made it extremely clear when speaking to the media around that time that my heart and soul had gone into playing for England and my empathy was with my national side and not with West Indies, even though of course I had huge admiration and respect for them.

Elsewhere in later editions of the magazine, my name was brought up around this precise point when David Gower wrote: 'I remember clearly the thrill of being asked to play for England for the first time, but I bet it meant no more to me than it did to David Lawrence.'

He was absolutely spot on about that.

The issue bubbled away for some time before the Frith and the Wisden management settled out of court with the players involved receiving a fulsome apology.

In my case things took an unexpected turn.

* * *

Unbeknown to me, the owner of the magazine at that time happened to be one of the richest men in the world and a huge cricket supporter, American tycoon John Paul Getty Jr. Getty was the heir to the oil baron John Paul Getty Sr, and he fell in love with the game to the extent that he put a lot of money into it in various ways.

Not only did he own Wisden, but he also installed a quite magnificent cricket ground in his sprawling estate at Wormsley, he served as president of Surrey CCC in 1996, and he helped fund ground improvements such as the Mound Stand at Lord's.

I took a phone call from his secretary who told me a little bit about Getty beyond what I already knew and then he said to me: 'Mr Getty is a great fan of yours and he knows that there is no way in the world that you wouldn't have given your everything when playing for England. He would like to apologise for what was written in the magazine in person and so he would like to invite you for tea with him at his private flat in London.'

Well, I was more than a little taken aback at the invitation, but gladly accepted. A few days later I found myself in Knightsbridge near Harrods and knocking on the door of this house which was opened by a butler. It was a nice place for sure, and I remember thinking I'd come a heck of a long way from Gloucester to be invited into a house by a butler, who looked like he was going to a wedding.I went in and was introduced to Mr Getty, who was fantastic. He couldn't have been more engaging and chatty and we sat down and had some tea.

The conversation was all about cricket and he explained why he was such a fan of mine. He liked my wholehearted efforts and the way I used to charge in and put everything into each delivery. He thought it was incredible how hard fast bowlers worked for their rewards and I told him it was bloody hard work!

He agreed that there would be no way I could do what I did if I wasn't committed totally to it. We talked about what was going on in the game and he really knew his stuff. It wasn't often that you spoke to someone with an American accent who had such a grasp of the game, so I asked him how his passion for it came about.

He told me about the struggles he'd had with drug addiction and how he had been getting himself cleaned up in rehab in the UK and while he was here he lived in St John's Wood. He told me that he was a massive baseball fan and loved the use of statistics and numbers in the game. During this period one of his neighbours happened to be Mick Jagger of the Rolling Stones, a dedicated cricket fan. Jagger would go around to visit him fairly regularly and when he did he would put the cricket on, much to Mr Getty's curiosity.

Jagger happily explained the game and its nuances to Mr Getty and he realised that it not only fulfilled his love of numbers and statistics, but it was also an enthralling spectacle in and of itself and that is where the devotion grew. The conversation continued and he asked about my injury and what had happened, and then he asked, 'So what are your plans now then if cricket is done for you?'

I hadn't really told many people at this stage, but I said that I had designs on opening a restaurant and that I had found some premises that I liked the look of. I had a bit of money ready to invest in the project, but I would need a bank to back me as well, so that was the next step. Without skipping a beat he handed me a card and said, 'Go and speak to the man on here from Schroders Bank, and tell him I sent you, see what he says.' I took the card having never heard of Schroders, but soon found out that they were a little bit more exclusive that NatWest and Barclays. I didn't really think much would come from my meeting but after laying out my business plan and detailing what I needed, they backed me completely and that is how I became a customer of Schroders Bank, along with Mr John Paul Getty Jr.

I remained with them for years and things worked out pretty well, and I subsequently found out that Mr Getty essentially paved the way by telling them to provide whatever I needed.

Our relationship continued beyond that meeting as Mr Getty then asked whether I might consider playing for his team in a game at Wormsley and even though I knew my days of professional cricket were over I thought I would still enjoy getting out on to the field if I could, so I agreed to play. I'd actually played another charity game before that with the Lord's Taverners in Cheltenham – the one and only game that I played alongside Andrew Symonds.

Symonds had played that summer for Gloucestershire and set the world on fire with his incredibly powerful batting, useful bowling and raw athleticism in the field. He was an incredible package and one that the county hoped would be a part of the furniture for 20 years, according to Jack Russell. The issue was that even though he was born in England, he emigrated aged just two with his adopted parents to Australia where he grew up and became as Australian as a kangaroo.

He had played Under-19 Cricket for Australia, but the fact he was born in England meant he could play for Gloucestershire as a local player rather than an overseas. He had tentatively suggested he had ambitions to play for England – to ensure the paperwork went through – but at the end of the season there was uproar. He was named the Cricket Writers' Club Young Player of the Year – the same award I received from Princess Diana – which is only open to England or potential England players, and then when he was selected for the England A side, he turned down the opportunity. Why? Because he was a fair dinkum Aussie and that is who he wanted to play for.

He went on to play for them many times, winning World Cups and Ashes series, an all-action all-rounder and someone who was tailor-made for the T20 circuit. Sadly he passed away at the age of

46 in 2022 following a car accident not long after his great friend Shane Warne.

He hadn't rejected England by the time we played in the charity game together, but his decision reignited the debate about who people play for and their motivations.

I admired his commitment to Australia and wanting to play for the country he knew and loved and where he had been brought up. Whatever your reason for making your choice, once you commit then that commitment shouldn't be called into question.

CHAPTER SIXTEEN

The Proprietor

Arriving back in the UK in 1994 with my professional cricket career at an end, I had some decisions to make about what I was going to do next. Fortunately time was on my side and I didn't have to rush into anything. I had had a good Benefit season that raised around £100,000.

And if there was one good thing to come out of how the injury happened, it was the fact that I had done it on England duty. The insurance policies playing for England and playing for Gloucestershire were a world apart. If I had suffered the same knee injury playing for Gloucestershire I would have received the bare minimum in terms of wages during my rehabilitation period and then once I retired I would have received a £15,000 insurance payout.

The fact that I was playing for England when the injury happened meant that I continued to receive England pay during my rehab and recovery, and then once I called it a day, the payout was £75,000. In fact it opened the eyes of the PCA to just how big the gap was for players and they set about changing the policies available to make sure that they were better looked after outside of the international set-up.

Players now are far better paid with more opportunities than at any time in the history of the game and the support around them is equally impressive, but it shouldn't have been down to dumb luck that I was injured playing for the right team that meant I at least left the game with something and could make a choice about my future.

In my heart I always knew that I wanted to run my own business and getting involved in hospitality and helping people have fun was something that I thought I would like and that I could do.

I loved going out and having a good time, and whenever I met bar or restaurant owners they made it look like the greatest gig in the world. I know now that the truth is far less glamorous and that it takes an incredible amount of hard work and support, but you learn as you go on.

Back in 1994 I didn't know anything about running a business, but I knew plenty about cricket and was an outgoing and chatty guy. I had done some cricket commentary and a few bits and bobs of other media work and as a result

I went on to feature as a guest presenter on local TV in a segment called 'Way out West', which was a bit like a local *One Show*. I would go and cover various activities in and around the South West, which was great fun. I remember once trying fencing and got fully kitted out with the mask and the sword – I thought I was d'Artagnan! Trying to wield it and land it on my opponent was another matter entirely though.

After the commentary work I did for Sky Sports on the World Cup while I was recovering from my first injury, I had stayed in touch with the producer and he asked whether I'd be keen to do a bit more. Sky had started to pick up a few more rights for cricket. They had the winter tours, some ODI cricket and highlights, plus the Benson & Hedges Cup and some Sunday League. There was enough to give me a real taste of this work, and while I enjoyed it up to a point, I felt like it wasn't really for me.

I thought the media activity would help me get through the disappointment that lay just under the surface at losing my cricket career, but actually it had the opposite effect. Every time I watched cricket, I couldn't help but think, 'I should be out there. If it wasn't for my knee I would be out there playing and performing.'

I started to feel quite bitter about the situation, like I had been robbed, and all those players who were getting to live out their dream on the field were having the fun that I should be having.

I'll be honest, this was a dark time for me and it took its toll.

Mentally, I struggled to cope. At the time, there was no real understanding of mental health issues in the wider public domain. The word mental was mainly used in a derogatory way, with stigma and shame attached to it. There certainly wasn't much empathy for people who found things mentally challenging.

Even now when we are much more aware of the subject, there is still an element of taboo about it and a reluctance for men especially to talk about these things. I look at sport and cricket in particular where we have amazing support from organisations such as the Professional Cricketers' Trust, who look after players going through tough times and were there to help around my injury.

They have been incredible in terms of support for so many players and their families, but even this is a relatively recent development.

I look at players who have been really brave in speaking out about their own struggles over the years. Whether it was Marcus Trescothick, Jonathan Trott or Ben Stokes, they have all shown that athletes are human and have the same problems we all face and it is okay to talk about it.

I didn't when I found myself dealing with what I can only describe as the grief of losing my career and my identity. I was Syd the fast bowler, the booming voice and lively character in the dressing room, ready to go into battle with my teammates. And then suddenly I wasn't any more.

And I wasn't ready for it.

I could and should have had professional help, but I didn't think I needed it. I kept telling myself I had nothing to worry about.

But deep down I didn't feel right. You would certainly call it anxiety. At times I felt depressed, but I can't say that it was depression for certain, which is a terrible affliction that friends of mine have struggled with and it can overwhelm you.

I don't know if that was the case with me, but there were times when I felt so lost and so down about things that I entertained some horrible thoughts.

I have not always looked after my mental health and have tried to find short-term solutions, usually in late night partying and trying to forget whatever issues I had. At times I was not great to be around and that affected those I loved the most. I was short-tempered and tetchy. And I just didn't want to be around people, which really isn't like me.

It was a downward spiral that might have swallowed me up were it not for the support of my family and friends, and then the realisation of a passion.

By 1995 I had made up my mind that I was going to try and open my own bar or restaurant, so I set about trying to work out how I was going to do it.

I spoke to friends who had managed and owned places in Bristol, I pored over literature about running a business and then thanks to the timing of my interaction with Mr Getty, I was able to secure the funding I needed to open my first venture, a wine bar and restaurant called Boom on Whiteladies Road.

I made sure I did my research and was as organised as I could be when it came to the nuts and bolts of staffing, suppliers and maintenance, but I was also happy to see what worked well elsewhere and bring it into my venue. Boom opened in 1996 following the Euros that were held in England, and it proved to be a good time to get into the trade.

The 1990s were a going-out decade that got stronger and stronger as the years went by and Boom was happy to ride that wave. Not that it was easy, mind you.

The restaurant business is hard work. Behind the scenes there is so much to get right and it is the most stress that I have ever experienced in my working life.

One of the best things I did was bring something I spotted in New York back to Bristol with me, which was to install big bifold doors so that in the summer they could be pushed wide open and the restaurant would feel like it was an outdoor venue. People loved that. Mine was the first restaurant in Bristol to do that and it proved really popular.

It was a great place that I ran for three years and really cut my teeth in the business. It was great to be able to host friends and of course the boys from Gloucestershire and the rugby and football clubs would come in. We would also often get visiting teams like Middlesex and Essex having their team dinners with us, which was always good.

But my vision of being able to kick back and relax with my friends was far from the reality of running a business like this. It was tougher than that. The first year was a real learning curve and like most businesses I made a loss, but in the second and third years it turned a profit and it was good fun in the process.

One New Year's Eve we had a party and I charged people £5 on the door to come in and at the end of the night we had about £750 in cash as well as our usual takings behind the bar and in the restaurant. That was a lightbulb moment for me because I realised

I could make money before anyone had even come in. It got me thinking about the nightclub trade. I would be making money just by people walking through the door and I could focus on the music, which was always my first love.

I started actively looking for a nightclub to invest in and around the same time the Po Na Na group came and made me an offer for Boom bar which made me a tidy profit and gave me the funds to get into the nightclub business.

The venue I found on Park Row was just what I was looking for. It had been a club before but had closed down and I thought I could really do something with it. It had an unassuming front entrance, just a single door leading down into the club, but once you got in it opened up to reveal a great party space where people could dance the night away.

I was lucky enough to be able to acquire the premises, and although it needed a bit of work, it had great potential. So in 1999 Dojo was born, bringing together my passion for music and for people to have a good time.

Just as I had done with Boom, I took inspiration from elsewhere and made it my own. There was a nightclub in London that Gaynor and I used to go to on a Monday night called Bar Rumba where Gilles Peterson would DJ, playing the kind of jazz- and funk-infused music that I love. So I wanted to try and recreate that sort of vibe in Bristol.

When I was a young man going out in Bristol in the 80s, I would often find myself on Park Row at a club called the Dug Out which was the spiritual home of the local music scene and that is where I made some great friends that helped me when I was starting out with Dojo.

I wanted the club to become as well-regarded as the Dug Out, and I wanted to give local DJs and artists the same sort of platform as they had back then. Some of the most well-known include the Wild Bunch, who became Massive Attack. They were always one of my favourite groups and they took their sound and skills all over the world to a huge audience, but they started in Bristol.

I had got to know Grant Marshall, one of the founder members, really well as we were often at the same bars and clubs when we were coming through in our respective fields.

The group went on to bigger and better things, but they never forgot their Bristol roots and they continued to DJ and appear locally. And Grant has always been good to me. Whenever they are on tour, there will be tickets for me to go along. I've think I've seen them about 10 times over the years and I've never had a bad night.

They were all part of a vibrant music scene in Bristol that also included drum and bass star Roni Size. I first met Roni way back at a youth club in Bristol and he had a cheekiness about him, but a warmth too and he has kept hold of that to this day.

When he was a kid he used to run around with a few friends who called themselves the 'Rock Mafia' and they had delusions of grandeur. They would sometimes hang around near the County Ground looking for ways to occupy themselves, and what is it that they say about idle hands? On a couple of occasions they got themselves into a bit of trouble by finding fun in throwing objects at windows and observing the reaction.

I'm not saying that I condone what they did, but the objects were nothing more than rotten apples that would splat across the window. Sometimes the homeowners would come running out of their houses to try and catch them, which they almost never did.

But when they were caught, Roni's quick wit and sharp tongue often got them out of a tight spot. When that didn't work, and the threat of a call to the police was made, he used his friendship with me to try and help, claiming that they were guests of mine at the game and it would be terrible to involve the police with the club. And luckily for him that did the trick as I vouched for them as good kids who would clean up the windows and not do it again. Having a Gloucestershire cricket player on your side around Nevil Road in the 80s still carried a bit of weight and Roni was glad of the connection.

We have kept in touch down the years and have stayed friends throughout. And he DJ'd a few times in the club, which always guaranteed a sell-out crowd. On one occasion it was so busy that he had to jump over a wall in the back just to get out.

We had so many fantastic DJs and musicians take control of the decks at Dojo down the years including Geoff Barrow from Portishead and Scott Hendy, Jazzy B from Soul II Soul, and one of my particular favourites, legendary DJ Kool Herc, who was a founding father of hip-hop back in the 1970s in the Bronx in New

York. Getting him to come over and play for us was one of the great triumphs of my time at Dojo, and the atmosphere in the club that night was simply sensational.

If only it could have always been like that. Unfortunately you have to take the good with the bad and in the night-time economy there are always going to be elements that make your life difficult.

I loved running my club, and I was fully hands-on and involved in every aspect, whether it was the music, the bar, the door or the maintenance. I wanted to be fully across everything, and for the most part I was. You would just as easily find me pouring a drink as you would with the marigolds on unblocking the toilet. No job was off limits, and I think my staff appreciated that approach. But running a nightclub is far from a straightforward occupation. That mix of youth, generally men and testosterone, plus alcohol, is enough to light a dangerous fire, and I've seen it many times.

That is because I worked on my own doors. I have always been involved on the door rather than just in the office because that is where everything starts. If people come into your club in a good mood and feeling happy then they are likely to have a good night and stay happy. If there are stresses and issues on the door, then they will bring them into the club.

For the first few years I would work on the door with some great guys and people knew me and my former career as a cricketer. But I would say over our last 10 years, most of the people coming into the club would have had no idea that I used to be a cricketer and have no idea that I owned the place either.

They see a big burly black guy on the door and they just assume that you are security staff, which leads to some interesting treatment from some people. Imagine their surprise when I tell them they can't come in and they are rude or abusive and demand to see the manager or the owner.

I tell them: 'He's not going to be very happy that you're insisting on seeing him, when I've given you a full explanation of why you can't come in.'

And yet they insist, so I do as they ask, and the look on their faces when I introduce myself as the proprietor is something I do miss. They weren't the only people who would be surprised that someone like me was running a business like Dojo.

The number of times that drinks reps from the big companies would come to the club looking to get their bottles into our fridges or to sell other products and would make a beeline for my manager James Phillips rather than me, thinking he was the proprietor. There just weren't many Black-owned businesses in the centre of Bristol, so assumptions were easily made.

We had a good crew working on the doors in the early days, led by Sean Viera and Phill Allen, two great guys. Sean was a champion kickboxer who is now a Team GB kickboxing coach, and his Elite Security team could handle anything.

I would enjoy spending time on the door with them and working out if there were people who couldn't come into the club due to their condition. Our view was that people were out to have a good time and we wanted to help them have the best time possible. If someone was going to run against that vibe then we didn't want to spoil things for the rest of the partygoers. And thankfully most people could understand that logic.

Dealing with the nightclub scene has its dangers, of course. But we generally had very little trouble inside the club. We would quickly remove anyone who was causing a problem, but I think we managed to create the right atmosphere from the off.

On occasion I would find myself dealing with one or two clients in the club who had crossed a line and needed to be taken out. I didn't mind doing it myself even though I had security for that.

A few times I would pick people up and carry them up the stairs and chuck them out before they knew what had happened. Sean would turn to me and say, 'Syd, why are you doing that?! Why didn't you radio us to come down and sort it.'

My reply would be, 'Well I've sorted it now, so no bother'. Sean and his team were great though. They dealt with things very professionally, and in 2007 when I told them that I had agreed to get in the ring for a charity boxing match, they were absolutely thrilled and offered to train me up for the fight. I fought a guy called Andrew Penn, a former New Zealand cricketer, and thanks to my training with Sean, it wasn't much of a contest. I was so ready for the fight that I practically ran out of my corner to get stuck in, and I was too much for him to handle. The fight didn't last long as I totally dominated him, but thanks to a disqualification I lost the fight. I

145

was so focused on getting the job done, I didn't hear the referee telling me to break and so I kept fighting. When my opponent hit the canvas I thought I'd won the fight, but apparently I ignored the referee and was disqualified.

The crowd turned on me and I think they felt a bit sorry for Andrew. He vowed he wouldn't be trying it again. At least we helped raised more than £14,000 for Sparks charity.

Back at the club I definitely think that things started to change in terms of the vibe after about 10-12 years for a few different reasons. My view was that the club was all about the music and it was very much focused on funk and soul.

And I had a real connection with most of the people who came to the club, and it sounds like a cliché, but I felt I knew everyone. Over time though that familiarity lessened.

People in my generation were going out less and less, and as the audience became younger their tastes also changed. We found ourselves catering to more of a garage and drum and bass crowd. But in order to stay relevant and popular, you have to adapt and evolve with your audience.

We were one of the only places in Bristol that had a late licence that allowed us to stay open till 6am, so when other places closed at 3am, we would get another spike in numbers, but at that stage of the night it could bring other issues.

Over time, the increased use of knives as weapons in UK cities was something we had to be aware of and our priority was to keep everyone as safe as possible. We always had cameras, above the door primarily, but then we also introduced body cameras as well to protect staff and clients.

We used metal scanners to make sure people didn't come in with hidden weapons, but you have no control over what happens outside your doors. There were instances when rival gangs would clash in the streets outside the club and the results could be very ugly. Everybody wants to be a gangster. But there are actually very few. There are lots of plastic gangsters but very few real ones. I would admit that a few of the real ones would find their way to my bar and then to my club and I didn't mind their custom at all, as long as things stayed within the right vibe in our space. Being known as a good-time venue and a place where the vibe was almost always a happy one was crucial in keeping trouble at bay and because I always treated people with respect. I think they had the same approach with me.

Even so, there were some nasty moments on our doorstep which sadly came with the territory. One guy got stabbed in the back during a fight near the club and was crippled as a result. You don't go into the nightclub business to see that. Another guy got slashed across the face quite badly, which was just horrible. Thankfully people could feel safe in our club and that is something I now look back on with pride. People might be shocked at some of the things that go on, but a Saturday night outside a nightclub in a major UK city can be an edgy place.

I had the club for 25 years, which is a long time for any venue to trade, and believe it or not we used to stay open till 9am for a time.

When 24-hour licensing came in, I applied straight away and so we tried a new idea where one night we opened at 10pm and then shut at 3am. We would have a tidy up and then we would open again for after parties from other clubs and stay open until 9am. I did that for a year and then had to put an end to it because it was too stressful and exhausting. The money was good, but it was just too hard to keep working to that schedule, and I didn't actually enjoy it.

What I did enjoy was seeing the positive impact the club could have on people, especially those young people who worked for me, behind the bar and managing the venue. I was always happy to give people a chance, and if someone was recommended to me by a friend I trusted, well that would mean more than anything else.

I employed people from all backgrounds, but I always had a good number of people from the African-Caribbean community working for me because I had lived that experience and knew that opportunities were not always easy to find. Most people who worked for me really enjoyed their time at Dojo and I am still friends with a lot of them, wherever they are in the world.

Alistair Baker worked for me at Boom and then Dojo and has gone on to achieve so much as a rugby coach and mentor, but he had his moments as a young lad. I don't know what I'd do without him and his support now. And the reason that he is able to help me as much as he does, driving me around and looking after me, is because of support from a friend he met at Boom called Alex Hartley. He has made a huge success of his life and he now lives in Hong Kong, but when he was younger and working at Boom things spiralled out of control and I was happy to lend some support to help him through it. Now he is helping Ali to help me, and I love that. Just trying to be there for each other in our hour of need.

I only mention these examples because it shows the positive impact we can all have on each other and you never know when the love that you put into the world will come back.

I opened Dojo because I loved seeing people have a good time and I think people forget just what powerful and positive places nightclubs can be. So many venues have closed down over the years and most fail to reopen.

Where are our kids and young people supposed to go and enjoy themselves if we keep removing the places where they have always had fun?

I have got several friends who met their wives and husbands at Dojo and now have kids who would love a Dojo of their own to go to. That is what I got into the business for. To bring people together with music and love. That is what makes me happy.

The nightclub game is fantastic, I would never knock it, even though my wife would worry about me until I came home safely.

Following the Covid pandemic we had actually decided to convert Dojo from a nightclub into a cocktail bar and stop opening quite so late.

We ran it like that for about a year before my health meant that I had to call it a day and bring the shutters down on my second career.

The rewards for the best cricketers in the world now are so great that there will be plenty of guys who will be able to retire and enjoy life without having to find another job or start a business, and that is great. But for all the players I played with and against, that was never an option.

Some are lucky enough to stay in the game as coaches or administrators or in the media, while lots walk away completely and do something totally different. Finding something that fills the gap of high-level competition and the adulation of a crowd is the biggest challenge though. I have to admit that I was lucky. I played cricket because I enjoyed it and then I got into the hospitality game and I enjoyed that too.

But when it came to filling that gap.

Something else came calling.

CHAPTER SEVENTEEN

Working Out

From about the age of 16 I have always done weights in the gym. It has been a constant part of my life for nearly 50 years, and I've loved it. When I used to do weight training and play cricket, I was constantly told, 'Oh you can't do weights, that's no good for you. You'll be too muscle-bound to bowl properly'.

Of course as time has gone on, I don't know a cricketer, let alone a bowler, who doesn't have some kind of weights programme built into their training regime.

Like anything it is all about what exercises you are doing and for what purpose. But to say that weight training has no place in a fast bowler's training plan is just naive.

When it comes to sport and something like bowling, we are all built differently and we all require different methods to strengthen different parts of our body or our physique to aid our technical work.

No two fast bowlers are the same and so no two training plans should be the same. We all offer different skills that can complement each other and covering as many bases as possible is the art of selection.

You will often hear about teams looking for a 'balanced attack' which is about giving a captain a different range of options that can be used as the game wears on and as conditions evolve, and also to combat the different strengths and weaknesses of the opposition.

My assets were pace and endurance – an ability to put batters under pressure and on the back foot at the start and end of the day and anywhere in between.

To do that I had to be fit and strong. I had to be able to withstand the extreme pressures that I was putting on my body through the unnatural action of bowling.

Even someone lithe with the physical attributes that James Anderson has been blessed with has to put their body through the wringer, over after over.

Both he and Jofra Archer might make it look as if bowling at pace is the easiest thing in the world, but it isn't. Even for guys like that who appear to glide towards the crease and send down magical ball after magical ball, the toll on their body is real and it hurts.

They are sprinting to the crease, jumping into the air, rotating their body to one side and then pushing huge forces through their joints in order to propel the ball towards the batter.

They then have to turn their body and get off the pitch as soon as possible, before walking back to their mark and doing it over and over again.

Now if you compare the frames of Anderson and Archer to someone like me, there is a huge difference in how we go about our work.

I didn't glide to the crease, I pounded my way in as fast as I could. I didn't take a small hop as I bowled, I took a leap and often moved my body out and away from the stumps for that extra bit of pressure. And then I contorted myself as the energy and forces I was exerting tried to escape from the various pinch points around my body.

I look at the level of professionalism in the game now off the field and it is a world away from the way things operated in the 80s and early 90s. I mentioned that Graham Gooch was a big proponent of fitness work, and he really did lead the way in that regard.

When I look at the strength and conditioning work that players do now and the resources that are available to them, that is something I am jealous of. Not so much the money and the wages, but the facilities and the support that is there.

I actually tried to bring some of this thinking into the game in 2005, but people didn't want to know. I had qualified as a personal trainer and I believed I was uniquely positioned to work in the game as a strength and conditioning coach with my fitness and training expertise combined with my bowling experience. I wrote or spoke to 16 out of 18 counties about offering support in this area and only a handful replied to me and they all said no. Now every team has someone in that position, but I couldn't get my foot in the door to begin a conversation about working in the game.

Even though I had made it to the top and was renowned for my strength and durability when I played, the knee injury apart, for some reason clubs were not interested.

I would love to be a player now with the amount of care that is provided for them to become the absolute best they can be. The way that fast bowlers like Jofra and Mark Wood are looked after is just brilliant, and in the case of Stuart Broad and Jimmy Anderson, they were able to produce their best performances in an England shirt rather than for their counties.

Bowlers in my era and before just had to play game after game and often bodies broke down because of that workload. Whereas for the modern player, there is much more thought as to what cricket they will play.

Of course there is far more international cricket now than ever before so the demands are still huge, not to mention the extra work in the IPL or other leagues. But even the most in-demand players have more control over their schedule than before, and you can always choose when to make yourself available and which contracts to sign. The power belongs to the players these days when it was anything but when I played.

And if you're going to play lots of cricket all around the world then you've got to be fit and strong and robust enough to deal with the workload, and that is where proper training and physical conditioning is so important.

That was my view throughout my career and I just agreed to disagree with the older players who said I would be too stiff and rigid if I did weight training.

They told me I needed to be supple and fluid in order to bowl fast, and I do understand where they were coming from. I know that bowlers like Michael Holding and Bob Willis focused on their aerobic fitness and strength in their legs to get themselves in shape for bowling. And going back further, Fred Truman would say that nothing got you fit for bowling better than bowling!

What works for you works for you. But I believed that the weight training along with the other aerobic and physical work that I did was going to help me by giving me the strength to cope with the demands of my action. When I felt strong and had trained hard, then I had the confidence and the power behind me to bowl fast. That was my point of difference. When I hadn't done the training and tried to bowl fast, I could tell the difference, so I just stuck to it and kept myself in good condition. Once I retired from the game for the second time in 1998, I still continued to train at the gym and look after myself because it was a way of life for me.

I enjoyed both the physical aspect of working out and the benefits it gave me and I also enjoyed the camaraderie and the community at the gym where you meet people with a similar interest as you but they can be from totally different backgrounds or be into completely different things outside of the gym. It is a great melting pot of people and I made some terrific friends over the years, many of whom have been utterly brilliant since my diagnosis.

For a few years I was happy going along to the gym and pushing myself in a variety of ways, but I hadn't taken it any further. I had some friends who were into proper bodybuilding, and I went along to their shows every now and again to support them, but I had no desire to get involved myself.

While training with them I would often get compliments that I already looked like a bodybuilder and it wouldn't take me long to get up to speed, but I resisted.

The shift came when I moved gyms and landed at a place called Trojan. I immediately fell in love with the place and it became another family. The owner Matty and his mum Julie were the driving forces behind it, but they were happy to let me join in and foster that sense of community.

It is what you might describe as a spit and sawdust type of place, but that is often where the hardest work gets done and you soon realise that a gym is not about the building or the equipment, but it is about the people, and Trojan drew so many good people through the door.

And once they were in the workout space then the good times would roll. The music would be on, the laughter and words of support would be loud, and the sweat would be extreme.

There was no room for egos and posturing, it was about getting the hard work done. There were no short cuts, just a willingness to put the hours and effort in. There was no judgement about who was doing what, because rest assured, there was always someone stronger than you in that gym. We were about supporting each other rather than making anyone feel small.

Matty was brilliant. He would let me use the gym even before it was supposed to be open, throwing me a set of keys and telling me to lock up when I was done. I would go in there at some unusual hours after a night at the club or if I was getting ready for a competition.

Trojan was a place where I would bring people if they needed a bit of support in their life. It is amazing how training and working out can help people deal with whatever else is going on in their lives. I would happily bring people along to train with me as we worked out our problems.

There were some serious bodybuilders in operation from the outset, and I got to know them all pretty well. Guys like Mike Crew, Dan Barry and Dave Guest were all competing at various competitions and I found myself getting drawn into their world.

At the age of 46, I was at a competition supporting my friend Howard Thomas in Newport. Looking closely at some of the guys competing in the over-40s category, I had a thought – I'm in better shape than some of these guys! I started thinking that maybe I could give it a go and be successful at it.

I spoke to Howard who was massively supportive and said that he would put me in touch with a friend of his called Dom, who could get me prepared for a show if I wanted to give it a go.

The more I thought about it the more I realised that it was just the challenge I needed at the time. Things were going well with the club and life was good, but I needed something to push me again and this might be it. I told Howard I would do it once and that would be it. I thought I'd get myself into good condition and push the limits of what I could do, and then that would be that itch scratched.

I started training more seriously and put together a programme that would turn a good muscular body into a great one. The exercises became far more rigorous and specific and the discipline that goes into your nutrition is at another level entirely. I gave myself a year to get into shape before competing and that was as difficult a challenge as I had faced up to that point. It meant a new programme of weight training, much more specialised in terms of the areas of the body I worked on, and it meant a completely different approach to food and nutrition to make sure that I could look the very best I possibly could when I eventually got onto the stage.

I have a massive sweet tooth and have always enjoyed cakes and sweets, but I had to cut them out of my diet completely and become much more disciplined than I ever was as a cricketer. But this was a challenge I wanted and the more I got into it the more I enjoyed it.

My training week was full on and I would work my way down my body from top to bottom and back again. I would start with my chest on Monday where I was lifting 200lbs, then the shoulders on a Tuesday, work on the back on Wednesday, leg day was Thursday and then back to the chest on Friday. I would train for 90 minutes on each body part and then throw in a bit of cardio work as well.

The further out from the show, the heavier the weights I was lifting. This was my bulking up phase, trying to get my muscles and my body as big as I possibly could.

From six months out, it was about gradually tapering off. Lifting progressively lighter weights but doing more repetitions.

I might have started out doing 6-8 reps with the very heaviest weights, but as I got close to the competition I would be doing 16-20 reps with lighter weights that would create greater definition rather than size. But for all the training you do, the key to really looking good and standing out in competition is your diet.

For three months before the show you are on a strict regime where you are depriving your body of all the happy foods that might make you feel good but certainly don't help accentuate your muscles. Plenty of protein but fewer carbohydrates, which are the enemy of the bodybuilder because they make you bloated and lose definition in your muscles. This is the part of the bodybuilding life that is the hardest. The denial of food that your body is craving, but you know won't help. We all know when we get a bit hangry, and the difference a good meal can make. Well, I felt hangry for weeks and I wasn't much fun to be around at all. Eventually I got to the competition for the South West Over-40s and finally took to the stage in a pair of Speedos feeling very self-conscious and a little nervous.

This might come as a surprise to a few people, especially my former teammates at Gloucestershire who know me as a performer who loves the stage.

Not only did I love performing with a ball in my hand on the field, but I would also enjoy the attention when I got the chance to show off in other situations such as when we were part of a fashion show for a benefit do.

Everyone walked down the catwalk as if it were the last place on earth they wanted to be, but I strutted my stuff before pulling out some old-school breakdancing moves that brought the house down.

I knew I would love the bodybuilding stage too, but this was my first time and so a few nerves were understandable.I got on the stage to some fairly anodyne music, which was my first mistake, and then did my various poses across 60 seconds in front of a very supportive crowd. And it was that reaction from the crowd that flicked the switch and had me hooked. By the time I walked off I knew that I'd be back, whatever the result.

The judges placed me in sixth position, which was about right. I didn't have anywhere near the definition I needed in my legs and that cost me.

I was always going to be less impressive in my legs due to my injuries as a cricketer. They would never get to the size they could've been had I not had any issues, but they certainly needed to get a bit bigger and much more defined.

The extra challenge I had was that, while I wasn't in the Courtney Walsh or Curtly Ambrose league in terms of height for a fast bowler, I was pretty tall for a bodybuilder at 5ft 10in. Bodybuilders tend to be shorter, squarer and squatter figures, which helps to accentuate the muscles, creating a sort of optical illusion.

Of course Arnold Schwarzenegger showed everyone that you could be tall and broad, and now my aim was to try and take home the title next time around.

I knew I could improve across the board and I was determined to be even more disciplined second time round, but first I had to find those foods that I had been missing for so long and after the event I went straight to the chicken shop. I had two chickens and a side of chips, washed down with a pint of Coke. Momentarily I was in heaven.

CHAPTER EIGHTEEN

Gradual Improvements

I visited Trojan the other day. A friend of mine, Pete Rose, took me there to see some of the old faces who I had come to know as another family.

It was brilliant seeing so many people I used to spend so much time with at the gym. The only difference being that the last time most of them saw me, I was pulling some of the heaviest weights in the place, and now I can just about sit upright in my wheelchair.

Some were visibly shocked and saddened by my condition, which is why I hadn't been out and about too much since getting home. It is tough for me, but it is also hard for people when they see me.

Matty Hudd was there and he's been incredible in terms of the support that he's given me and the money that he and others have raised with charity events such as 'Cycle4Syd' where they did a relay on static bikes to cover the distance from Bristol to Sri Lanka, the opposition in my first Test match.

I always said that Trojan was a community and I feel like I have played my part in bringing people together over the years. This has been a chance for that community to wrap me up in return and they have done just that and more. I'm so grateful for their support, just as I was when I was competing in the bodybuilding competitions in the West and then beyond.

The only way to qualify for the national competition was to win your local area first and I was still a way off that, having come sixth at my first attempt.

It had been a huge challenge for me physically but perhaps more importantly mentally. Denying myself the food that I craved and working hard on bulking and then shredding my body.

I developed a plan for the second time round which involved another level of training, a rigorous attention to detail on my diet, and a fabulous backing track called 'Bad Boy Back Again' put together by DJ Dan Wild, who performed at my club.

Having music that I really loved behind me absolutely fed into my showman's personality which made for a better 60-second routine in front of the judges.

Being a bodybuilder I was searching for perfection that can never be found. The only thing to do is to keep trying to improve a little bit more every time you go to the gym or you work on some aspect of your training.

The endorphins and the pleasure that you get from seeing your body in terrific physical shape is so addictive. You just want more. And then when you get on stage and people are marvelling at you, that is a buzz all of its own, but the sacrifice is hard.

That is why only certain people can compete.

When you see someone up there on stage, you know they have put themselves through a 17-week diet from hell.

The second year I competed, I placed second in the South West, and I loved it even more than the first. The backing track was a huge hit and I had grown in confidence so that when I got on the stage I was responding to the crowd just like I did as a fast bowler. When they cheered, my flex and my poses became more defined and more impressive. I was loving it and wanted to do more.

Maybe it would be third time lucky. I left nothing to chance, bulking up more than ever between September and December with training sessions that pushed me to the limit. Christmas was quieter with my mind focused on looking after my body for the next year's competition and in January I began the diet that would make or break my chances.

I was eating mainly broccoli accompanied by chicken. Boring food. Egg whites, a bit of salmon, rice and green vegetables and minimal carbs until you cut them out entirely. In the last five weeks it is just fish. The carbs have gone and you have just a little bit of fibre to keep things moving. It is brutal.

But somewhere deep inside I loved it. Even though my moods were wildly fluctuating and I was generally no fun to be around due to being permanently hangry, I saw it as a challenge to overcome and something that I had control over. The fact that my cricket career was ended by something outside of my control had led to unresolved issues that were being met by bodybuilding.

It is hard to explain to people who have not played professional sport and then had that opportunity taken away from them. I missed the adulation, I missed the cheers of the crowd and until I started bodybuilding I thought I would never experience those things again. But that is what I got back when I climbed onto that stage and heard the crowd once more.

They were cheering, they were clapping, they were supporting you and you could feel the warmth. When I got on the stage I was a showman again, and I had missed that. I loved it, so putting myself through the pain of preparation was worth it.

Third time around I stepped onto the stage in Exeter full of confidence knowing that my body had never been in better shape, and the muscles I had developed had never been more defined.

Having done the preparation and denied myself so much in the build-up to the competition I felt like it was now or never for me. I liked my chances compared to the other bodybuilders alongside me and as they took to the stage one by one I felt more and more confident that I would be the man to beat.

Still though, you never know. There is still a level of performance required to show off your body as well as you possibly can. With another banging track behind me I delivered my best performance yet, nailing my poses and holding my form with the experience I had gained across the previous two years. After we had all performed our set, we were called onto the stage together to hear the results, and each time a position was announced I expected to hear my name, but it never came, until I was the very last name to be read out.

I had finally won the National Amateur Bodybuilding Association's West of England Over-40s competition and was going to compete at the British finals. I had achieved what I set out to do and I was thrilled. The crowd went wild, the whooping and cheering was incredible, and I couldn't wait to get my hands on the trophy.

This time the chicken shop visit would have to wait. I had six weeks to keep myself in prime condition before I took on the best in the country in Southport. Pushing myself against the best was going to be another fantastic challenge and one that I just wanted to enjoy. Of course I wanted to win too, but just getting to this stage was a massive achievement and everyone at Trojan clearly agreed.

We took lots of support from the gym to the competition; it seemed like everyone wanted to come along and be a part of it. That was the nature of our Trojan community, we all wanted to support each other so it meant that I had plenty of people shouting my name when I went up against the country's best. Word had got round the bodybuilding community about me and I think people were keen to see how this ex-cricketer had managed to transform his body. I had a lot of people coming up to me and asking me questions about my journey and after I had performed they were asking about my backing track too! They loved the music as much as I did.

Unfortunately, at my first attempt I didn't even place in the British Championships, which was another wake-up call for me in terms of how high the standard was. I still thought I could go a little better so I knew I'd be back and I set my mind to achieving even more.

Now I knew precisely what was required in terms of training and diet in order to compete with the very best and over the next two years of competition I managed to win the West of England title to qualify for the British competition, but I never quite managed to win the national crown. My best placed finish was fifth in 2015 in the Over-50s category, which really took some doing, but I couldn't quite get to the top of the podium.

Despite not winning the overall British title for the Over-40s or Over-50s, I still felt like it was a successful stint as a competitive bodybuilder. I continued to compete until 2019, making it eight years that I put my body and mind through the wringer to get myself into the best possible shape I could.

The grumpiness and mood swings that came with it at times were not much fun for those around me, especially my wife, but we got through it and came out the other side satisfied that I had got what I wanted out of it.

Up until I started bodybuilding competitively, something was missing from my life. I had been robbed of the second half of my cricket career and I felt quite down about it for years afterwards.

I know you shouldn't compare yourself to others but I couldn't help it. Even when I was pleased that my friends had succeeded there was still a part of me that believed it could or should have been me.

Devon Malcolm is a great friend of mine and we used to go out a fair bit together when we were younger. He was a terrific bowler and had real pace, as we saw on the international stage.

But when he had that memorable day against South Africa in 1994, as much as I was happy for him taking 9-57 at The Oval, there was a little voice in my head saying, 'That could have been me'. It was the same whenever one of the guys I knew well had a big day out. I was always wondering, what if? What if I hadn't had that injury? What if I had played in another 10 or 20 Test matches? Those questions slip away over time, but it is only natural to wonder what might have been had I managed to avoid serious injury.

I had always felt that in order to be considered a real Test player, someone who could say they had proven themselves time and again, you had to play 25 matches or more. That was always the number I had in my head and where I wanted to get to.

I didn't even manage half that number. Five Test matches is not a huge sample size to really say how good a player you were, no matter what you might think in your own mind.

If I had managed to stay fit then I'd like to think I would have played 25 matches, and maybe more. But we will never know.

That was a fire that burned deep inside me and it was taken away, so I looked for something else to take its place, and bodybuilding did that for me.

Was it worth it?

I think so.

CHAPTER NINETEEN

Living with MND

On June 21, 2024 I told the world I had MND. I didn't want to. I still had trouble fully accepting the diagnosis myself. If everybody knew, then there would be no escaping it. I was really never going to wake up from this nightmare.

I had already told those close to me, but this announcement with the support of the club and the PCA would be a big deal, and so it proved.

The outpouring of affection and messages of support were quite overwhelming, especially as I probably still wasn't quite ready to talk to the outside world yet. I received lots of messages from people who I hadn't been in touch with for years but who had been a part of my life at one point or another and that continues to this day and brings me great comfort.

Once I was back in my house and in a routine with my carers and my support, I began to start to think about when and how I would start to see more people. I wasn't hugely comfortable with lots of people coming to the house apart from my closest friends, and they really have been amazing. None more so than my friend and driver Alistair Baker, who has gone above and beyond for me and is like part of my family.

I first met Ali when he came to work for me at Boom. He was working in Bella Pasta next door and one of his friends was working as a chef in my kitchen and he came in looking for a job behind the bar. He was a good lad with a good heart and I hired him. We just got on well because he was happy to get stuck in and nothing was too much trouble. I like people who give life a go and will say yes to adventures and experiences and he was one of those.

Like a few of the guys who had worked for me over the years he had his up and downs with things at home and sometimes life was pretty tricky. You never know what people are going through, but it can have a debilitating effect.

A bar or a nightclub is often an easy place to forget your worries and just have a good time, but once the music stops and the drink wears off, the problems haven't necessarily gone anywhere. I knew that myself and so I never judged anyone who was going through a bit of difficulty and if I could help them in any way then I was always prepared to do so.

A lot of young men find it hard to find their place in the world and struggle to cope with pressures and expectations on them. Some just need a bit of extra support to get them to the next stage of life. If I could be someone that they could lean on or rely on at times then that is what I would do and Alistair was one of a several young men who needed that, but I wasn't a soft touch.

He moved away to Cheltenham for a time to try and get himself sorted, and when he came back I was running Dojo and offered him work while he completed his education. At times I had to set him right with a few home truths, but he wasn't the only one. I think a few guys got a bollocking off me down the years, but I only did it to help them out.

Just as I had been given the right support from people like Tony Brown and Viv Richards, I saw it as part of my responsibility to help others where I could, especially young men who found it difficult to get their life in order.

Ali certainly got his life on track and he has been so supportive of me since he heard the news, ready to take me wherever I need to get to. One of those places was Edgbaston for T20 Finals Day in 2024 after my beloved Gloucestershire qualified for one of the champagne days in the cricket calendar.

I spoke to the PCA and the club and made it clear that I would be getting along to support my team and would hopefully see them win some more silverware.

To have Mark Alleyne, my former teammate and good friend, back in charge as head coach was already a joyous thing in my eyes, but to see the immediate impact he was having on the team on the field made me so proud. The PCA were doing some fundraising on the day, and I wanted to support those efforts too. I know first-hand just what a difference the PCA can make to former players and their families during difficult times and I've seen the videos they produce to tell those stories, so when they asked if I would be prepared to be the subject of their next video, I was happy to help.

It meant a day of filming with Sky Sports at the County Ground in Bristol for an interview and video that would be shown during the live broadcast on Finals Day.

In the run-up to the day I was looking forward to it, but when the day actually arrived I was very anxious. It would be the first time that I'd be on camera since my diagnosis. I knew that for most people it would be the first time that they would have seen me for over a year and they would be surprised at the condition I was now in.

A few weeks before this I went to a players' reunion at the club and saw a few of my old teammates, who were pretty shocked to see the condition I was in. I was glad to have been able to do that in person with them, but their reactions told me what to expect when more people saw me like this.

The day began like it always does now with my carers coming in and getting me up, putting me in my chair and wheeling me to the shower room. They wash me and dry me and put me on the bed. They then dress me and sit me up ready for breakfast.

This is my routine and over time as I have gotten weaker I have relied on them for more and more. They do their job with a smile on their face and they always make me feel comfortable, and I am so grateful for the gentle grace in the way that they look after me.

On the days when I need to go out, like today for the Sky interview, Alistair comes round and gets me into my chair and then into the car. He lives in a flat overlooking the ground, so he knows exactly where to go.

When he drove me through the gates, I felt a huge wave of emotion because this was a place that meant so much to me. I was 16 years old when I first walked into the ground and it seemed so big and imposing. And as I got older, I grew to love the place and to see it as my second home.

I came in round the back so people didn't see me, which is absolutely not what I wanted when I became club president. For me not to have been there at all over the summer was a real shame. The first person I saw when we drove in was Andy Brassington, a former teammate of mine and another great friend who couldn't have done more for me.

We go way back to our playing days at Gloucestershire when I was first coming into the team and he was the first-choice wicketkeeper. We played a fair few games together before Jack Russell took the gloves on a permanent basis and Andy played for and mentored the second team with the odd appearance back in the firsts. He was a superb keeper, but a little less handy with the bat!

After he finished playing, Andy worked at the club in a marketing capacity before starting his own marketing and events agency that he's made a great success of. It was by using those skills that he was able to convene one of the best nights of my life later that year.

Here he was to support me and help me through my first TV appearance in a very long time. The Sky Sports camera crew were already there filming, waiting to capture my every move, and I was nervous and unsettled.

I waited in the car for a few moments before I took a deep breath and told Alistair I was ready to go. Even though I was nervous, I still wanted to do the interview. I didn't want to back out and turn away from what would be a huge challenge. The determination to take things on was still there.

As I was manoeuvred into position, seeing those lights in my face I was really conscious of every breath I took and how I spoke. I knew that people watching this would be taken aback and maybe they would feel sorry for me, and that is something I didn't want.

I know it is a normal human reaction to feel sympathy for someone in a worse situation than yourself, but the last thing I wanted was for people to start treating me differently. I am still Syd. In my head and in my mind, I am the same person. It's just that my body doesn't work as well as it used to.

* * *

I get out of the van and make my way round the back and into the pavilion, to the room where we are going to do the interview. I am feeling quite anxious but Alistair is there to reassure me and to give me water because my mouth is so dry. Over the last few months my voice has really started to falter. It is getting harder and harder for me to speak with anything like the volume I used to. My muscular body and my confident voice were my calling cards for years. They were a huge part of who I am, and they have both been gradually taken away from me.

I am determined to do this interview though, and let people know about my situation. The lights go on and the questions come, and I am filled with energy to tell my story. I take my time and get the words out as I want to, and the microphone is there to pick things up clearly. And once we're done, I feel like it has gone pretty well. The producer and the cameraman are happy with what they've got, and I am looking forward to seeing the finished film. That will come on T20 Finals Day, which is another event I'm looking forward to.

I get home from the ground and I'm knackered. I feel like I've bowled 20 overs uphill, so I sleep well that night and rest up the next day too.

Saturday rolls around and I'm really looking forward to seeing my team play at Edgbaston. But I'm nervous about being in front of such a big crowd for the first time since my diagnosis. I've got Alistair driving me and my son Buster to the game, as well as a couple of Buster's mates who are up for a day out, but before we can go I've got to go to the toilet. And such was my anxiety I had to go again before we get on the road.

I had tried to prepare myself as best I could for the day but I sleep all the way there and I'm woken when we get to Edgbaston. We arrive during the first semi-final between Somerset and Surrey and make our way immediately to the side of the pitch.

I have agreed to appear on the big screen along with former Hampshire and England spinner Shaun Udal, who is dealing with Parkinson's.

We are there to show where the money for the Professional Cricketers' Trust goes, to highlight the sort of things and people the PCA supports. While I'm waiting on the side with Buster, I get a sudden wave of emotion and I don't want to go out onto the field. It is a full house at Edgbaston and we are right by the Hollies Stand.

It is all a bit overwhelming for me and I shed a few tears.

Buster is brilliant though. He knows me and knows it is just a wobble. We have a bit of a chat and he wipes my eyes, and tells me I can do it.

Once the game is finished I wheel myself onto the ground and there is a hugely warm reception for both Shaun and me, which makes me feel good.

We have a chat on the big screen and then Daniel Norcross from the BBC comes over and interviews me for *Test Match Special*. Once it was done I just wanted to get off and get away from all the eyes on me. I had said my piece and I had done okay, but now I just wanted to disappear. I was totally out of my comfort zone and just didn't feel like I did when I played in front of big crowds.

I was taken up to the PCA box where people were busy working on the charity aspect of the day, as well as others enjoying the cricket.

I've got a great spot looking out on the ground with the windows fully open, so it feels like we are outside. I lean my chair back and settle in to watch the cricket. Gloucestershire are outstanding. The bowlers are just brilliant as they bowl Sussex out f0r 106 before chasing down the target to win by eight wickets.

We have never won the T20 Cup before and now we are in a final, and I am absolutely delighted to be there as the club's president, as a former player and as a Gloucestershire fan.

While the semi-final is taking place, Nick Hoult from *The Telegraph* comes up to interview me and talk about my career and living with MND. The more awareness and support we can get for this cruel disease the better, and hopefully one day we will find a way to treat it and cure it. More time, money and research is required, so I am happy to do my bit.

In between the innings my former teammate and one-time roommate Mike Atherton comes to visit me. Not for an interview, but just to say hello and have a catch-up. It is already a special day.

As the final gets underway, my son asks me how I'm doing as this is already the longest I've been out the house since I got home from the hospital. I'm a little tired but I'm fine and I want to see how the boys will get on, especially as the final is a West Country derby with Somerset.

Just then I hear the TV commentary. They have panned up to me in the box as they have done a few times and Ian Ward says: 'There's Syd Lawrence, no doubt a very proud Gloucestershire president. It has been a long day and with his current situation he may not be around to the end to see if his side can get over the line…'My reply is instant: 'Nonsense! I'm not going anywhere! You must be joking.' It is about as loud as I have been in months.

I don't know what the impact will be on me, but I know I am going to watch my team win or lose. I want to be there at the end.

Boy, was I glad to have stayed. They put on another masterful performance, again stifling the opposition batters so that Somerset can only post 124.

It shouldn't be enough, but you never know in a final. Pressure can do funny things to players. I shouldn't have worried. Miles Hammond and Cameron Bancroft put on 112 for the first wicket and the game is done and dusted in emphatic style. Another eight-wicket win.

At the end of the game, captain James Bracey is given the trophy and he starts to head over to the stand below me. The next thing I know he has climbed up over the railings and through the window and he has put the trophy in my lap for me to hold.

It is a moment I will never forget. I am so proud of the team for achieving something really special and for doing it their way with Mark at the helm. And for them to include me in this way as part of their celebrations just got me, and the tears started again. I will always be so grateful to James for that moment, and having spoken to him since, I know it was a hugely emotional moment for him too.

The images of him doing that were across most of the newspapers and websites the next day and it probably gave the occasion a little extra poignancy, but there is something really important to remember.

As much as I enjoyed being there and supporting the team, it was not about me. I had my time playing and competing on the field, so I know what goes into it.

That day was all about the players and the staff who worked so hard to get a shot at glory and then were able to take it with their skill and quality of cricket. They were the players wearing the Gloucestershire badge, as so many of us have done down the years, but it is their time and the focus should be on them.

It was a long day for sure and unsurprisingly I fell asleep on the way home, but before I did I looked across the car at Buster and we shared a smile and a nod, and that is what made the day so special for me. Not only did I get to watch my team win a trophy, but I got to do it with my son at my side. It is a moment that would have been experienced by so many parents and children over the years at stadiums up and down the country, watching cricket, football, rugby and other sports, and I got to enjoy that feeling with my son. That is what I wanted more than anything else and I was lucky enough to experience it.

I'm absolutely knackered and I need to get my rest, because after such an emotional day I have another one coming up at the end of the following week. It's Buster and Alice's wedding and I need as much energy as I can muster for that one.

CHAPTER TWENTY

Family and Friends

My physical deterioration over a number of months has been a painful experience. I have got weaker and weaker and I can do less and less. First it was the removal of the ability to move myself from one place to another, then it was things like being able to wash myself and use the toilet.

The ability to hold a knife and fork and bring food and drink to my mouth then started to wobble until it became impossible.

Holding the TV remote control was another small thing that gave me some independence and now that has gone too.

I needed some help getting extra oxygen into my lungs at night, so I had a machine to help me with that. I now require that help during the day too.

More and more has been taken away from me, bit by bit. I knew this is what I had to look forward to, but the reality is far more painful than what I even imagined.

And yet, I consider myself lucky. Why?

Because each and every step of the way I have had the constant love and support of my wife Gaynor. From the day we first met, I have been the lucky one.

Like any couple that go through life together, it is never going to be sweetness and roses all the time, but we have had a great time together. If you can have someone along for the ride and there is love between you, then you can get through anything and be stronger for it.

From the moment I went into hospital for the initial tests, it has been tough on Gaynor, who has had to cope with the same uncertainty as me, but also the way I have reacted to things.

Throughout it all she has been the wife I knew she would be. We have cried a lot, but we've also laughed and shared lots of memories that will keep her going when I'm gone. We have done so much together and this is one more thing that we get to share as a family and we are determined to make it as positive as we can.

I first met Gaynor at the Avon Gorge hotel in Bristol. I was there with Barrie Bridle, who had played a bit of second-team cricket at Gloucestershire and was one of the sons of our head groundsman, Dave Bridle.

He and I had become really good mates and we still are, even though he now lives over in Australia. I was with him at this event and Gaynor walked in and just blew me away. I had seen her before and thought she was absolutely stunning, but I didn't have the balls to talk to her.

This time I was sure I would change that, and such was my state of mind I turned to Barrie and said: 'I am going to marry that woman.' I was smitten.

I went over to speak to her and it turned out she was there with her girlfriends, and they were spying on her ex-husband. We had a brief chat and I found out where she would be going later.

We then met at another club that night and that is where we started to get to know each other. I asked if I could take her out on a date. She agreed, and the rest is history.

That history also contains some rocky times when we drifted apart and were not that happy. And in the late 1990s we actually split up for about four years.

She had lost her dad and I was dealing with my failure to come back as a cricketer while also trying to get my wine bar off the ground, which wasn't easy.

There was a lot of stress in our lives and I admit that I wasn't the best partner I could have been at that time.

We split up but promised we would be responsible parents and put our son Buster first. So we continued to do things together as a family, even going away on holiday so that neither of us would miss out on those moments with him.

Over time we grew closer again and the love that was always there came to the fore, but we didn't want to get back together for the sake of Buster. If we were to resume our relationship, then it would have to be because we wanted it for each other, first and foremost. If we were only doing it for him, then we would find ourselves in trouble.

Despite being together for a long time and having a son together, we didn't actually get married during that period. When we got back together for the right reasons after our split, we knew it would last and so we decided to make it official. We got married in 2004 with all our friends and family around us and it was a magical time. We also went back to Jamaica for our honeymoon at Sandals which was just a brilliant trip for the two of us and one that immediately brings a smile to my face when I think about it.

Having a partner you can rely on is a wonderful thing and I have been so supported through this period in my life. I could not have faced this cruel disease on my own, and I am so lucky to have Gaynor by my side.

The same must be said of my son Buster, who has been nothing short of incredible. Both his mum and I are so proud of the man he has become and I feel lucky to be his dad.

We have always been close. Our love of sport has been a natural bonding agent across his life, but so too has been our enthusiasm for music and for people. Buster is less of an extrovert than me, but such is his character and his willingness to face a challenge that he has become hugely impressive in the way he carries himself and looks out to the world.

He has become a father to our beautiful grand-daughter Maya and he brought forward his wedding to our gorgeous daughter-in-law Alice so that I could not only attend the ceremony but make a speech and embarrass him with love as any dad would want to.

Their plans for a grand wedding in 2025 were shelved, sacrificing their big day for me and having a much smaller, more intimate affair with around 20 guests. I can never thank them enough for allowing me to be such an integral part of their plans, and I hope the speech I made was just the right side of the line when it came to embarrassing poor Buster. I don't think he would have expected anything less though.

I won't go into the details of such a private moment, but needless to say he knows just how much I love him and that will never change.

I was nervous at speaking in front of our family and friends. My anxiety was through the roof because my voice had become so weak so quickly and I didn't want to make a fool of myself and spoil the day. Those fears are always worse before the event, but the loss of my voice has been the most difficult to take because it is such a part of who I am.

The day itself was brilliant, and I am so grateful to both Buster and Alice for helping us create memories that will live on long after I'm gone. The only downside came in the weeks afterwards when I took a turn for the worse and needed to go back into hospital for a couple of weeks. Essentially, I was suffering from exhaustion because the events had taken so much out of me and I was really struggling to recover. I couldn't get enough oxygen into my body and I was shutting down.

I rested and recovered well enough to return home, and it served as a reminder of just how far my physicality had fallen. I would need to be more careful with what I did in the future.

I am so pleased at how close Buster and I are because that wasn't the sort of relationship I had with my dad. We loved each other, but it was a much stiffer and more distant relationship, which I think most children brought up in Caribbean households pre-1980 could identify with. I was always a mummy's boy and I wasn't that close to my dad until he was ill at the end of his life. He died from cancer a few years after my mum passed away and we spent a lot of time together, talking a lot more than we ever did when I was growing up.

It was special to be able to share that time with him at the end, and for Buster too, who was able to help nurse him a little. My dad was a bit Victorian in his approach, which I think most Caribbean fathers were in those days. They found it hard to express themselves beyond the basics. He went to work and earned his money for the family, as did my mum as a nurse, and with four daughters and two sons we all had to find our way. With Buster I wanted to take an active role in his life and I think I managed it, even coaching him cricket at school.

We were fortunate enough to be able to afford to send him to Colston's Primary School and try to give him all the opportunities that I didn't have growing up. That is the nature of aspiration and trying to provide more for your kids than you had.

I was asked if I would help out with cricket coaching one afternoon a week in the summer which I was happy to do, and then once Buster was on the cusp of entering the senior school, they asked whether I would be interested in becoming a more involved cricket coach and working three days a week.

I enjoyed the coaching for sure, but the fact that we would receive a useful discount on Buster's fees also helped in my decision-making! I coached the school first XI for eight years and took them on a cricket tour to Grenada in 2009, which was a brilliant trip and their first tour abroad as part of an increased focus on cricket at the school.

Lots of public schools had been there on cricket tours before us, but the locals found it very strange to see a man with Caribbean heritage in charge. I was quite happy to change their outlook on that.

Buster was a part of that tour, but he had already decided that his future didn't lie in cricket and that he was going to concentrate on rugby. He was a useful cricketer, a strong all-rounder, and he played for the county age-group sides, but he was a fabulous back-row rugby player and he found it more appealing.

During one of his games for Gloucestershire he had been hit for a few runs and then he was bowled out cheaply and as he made his way off another kid gave him a bit of a send-off and told him, 'You'll never be as good as your dad'. After that game he came up to me and said that he didn't want to play cricket any more and he wanted to focus on rugby.

If that is what he wanted to do, then fine by me. Following in your father's footsteps is something that a lot of sportsmen do, but it does come with a bit of pressure that others don't have. So I totally understood if Buster didn't want to do that. I told him he could still enjoy cricket and play for fun, alongside his rugby, which is what he ended up doing.

He gave rugby a good go, playing professionally for Wasps in 2014 either side of two spells at Birmingham Moseley and then at Rotherham Titans.

I was so proud of his own sporting career and going along to games and watching him perform was one of my favourite things to do. As too was training with him and having him come and work in the club when he was old enough. Those are the simple pleasures that I will treasure.

Over the years we have talked about some of the experiences I have had when it comes to racism and how I dealt with it. Buster has a different view to me, or at least he did during a period of relative calm before some people became emboldened to let their hate spill forth.

We would talk about the subject of 'banter' in the dressing room, particularly after hearing a couple of his teammates refer to him as 'blubbery lips'. I told him nicknames like that were not on. He shouldn't stand for it. He said, 'Dad, you don't understand, it is just banter'. But I don't think it is. When people are mocking you for your features, it crosses a line. We have bigger noses, we have bigger lips, why is that something to take the mickey out of? He wouldn't have it though. We had to agree to disagree on that one.

Buster is a proud young man, but he says he doesn't see colour. And as a mixed-race man, he is living an experience I never had and he is able to enjoy the best of both worlds at times too.

But unfortunately I think we all see colour and the world doesn't work in the way Buster would like it to. Working in the nightclub he saw it all. He said the Black kids used to give him a hard time because he was mixed race. But once people got to know him, he would win everyone over, he is that kind of guy.

Seeing your son interacting with other staff and clients in a way that reflects well on him and the way we have brought him up is a lovely thing. He was a popular guy even if he was a little shyer than I was.

We trained together plenty of time during my bodybuilding days and beyond. I just about had him covered on the weights, but not by much. He is a seriously strong boy. We even competed together at the Superhuman Games in Bristol and placed in the Top 10. That was so much fun and one of the best days we've had together. I know I'm his dad and he's my son, but he's also my best mate.

The professional rugby career gradually came to an end a few years ago and he has since trained as a qualified electrician and is working on some great projects.

The main thing though is that he is happy with his family who are the centre of his world. He has made lots of adjustments to find time to be there for me during this disease and I can't thank him enough for it all, but there was one moment that stood out.

Thanks to Andy Brassington, a charity dinner and fundraiser was held for me and the PCA Trust at the home of Bristol City. There were hundreds of friends and former teammates from across my life – in Gloucester, in Bristol, in sport, in hospitality, in fitness, and many other places, with some travelling from across the world to be there. It was the most emotional evening of my life and something that was a bit overwhelming, but utterly fantastic and appreciated.

Nothing though, gave me more joy than watching and listening to my son deliver a knockout speech on the night. He just blew me away with his clarity, his elegance and his poise. You could have heard a pin drop as he spoke, and then the applause for him was immense.

A lot of the people in that room will have known him all his life and others will have been listening to him speak for the first time, and in the days and weeks after the event, people were still telling me how powerful his words were.

I have never been more proud of the young man he has become.

Compared to how I am now, I felt quite strong and robust at the wedding, and then later at the dinner in my honour. That night was something else. How can I describe an event where so many people turn up to support you and tell you they love you and raise money to help try and beat this horrible disease.

And yet the elephant in the room is the fact that for many of them, it will be the last time they see me. For many it is a chance for them to say goodbye, because this disease is going to take me.

So while it was a truly uplifting and positive event brilliantly run by Andy and his team, there was also an incredible amount of sadness in the room.

I am not afraid to show my emotions. And neither was anyone else after I managed to make a speech and thank them all for coming. If the ability to make people cry was a sport, I would be an Olympic champion.

There were messages on the big screen from friends who couldn't make it such as Sir Viv Richards and Courtney Walsh, and we had some fun listening to Jack Russell, Devon Malcolm and Phil Tufnell tell some stories about our more youthful days.

David Fulton – one of the Kent batters who persuaded me that my time as a bowler was up – did a terrific job as the host to help make it a night to remember. And we raised over £100,000 for charity too.

Seeing so many people from across my life was a strange experience, but it reminded me of moments and events that helped shape who I am to this day. There were guys from Gloucester City Cricket Club as well as Bristol West Indians who I also turned out for in my early days.

Having only played a handful of second XI games in 1980 and with one or two unfortunate experiences, my formative years at Gloucestershire were a little mixed. The truth is that I was quite lonely and didn't immediately fit in, which had been a familiar story at club level and in junior representative cricket. My ability carried me through and eventually I would find friends.

I went through the same process at Gloucestershire, but one thing that did help was when my brother-in-law, Ronald, who was married to my sister Bev, asked if I wanted to come along with him to the Bristol West Indian Cricket Club.

I'd heard of them but didn't have a connection until Ronald. I visited with him and the vibe was just right with plenty of noise and life on and off the field.

I was introduced to a few people and the question everyone asked was whether I would be able to play for the club on the weekends when I wasn't playing for Gloucestershire. I certainly wanted to but I knew I would have to check with the club first. When I asked if I could, the response was muted to say the least. Not for any sinister reason I don't think, but because they played in a league a few tiers lower than Gloucester City and there was some concern as to whether the quality of cricket would be good enough.

Well, considering I was hardly getting a game in the Gloucester City first team, I argued my case. There was a bit of hand-wringing about it but eventually the club agreed that I could turn out for them.

I really enjoyed my time playing there. It was so much fun in a dressing room that was full of laughter and jokes, with a Caribbean twist. The language was colourful, not with swearing, but with an eclectic richness and turn of phrase. It was quick and quick-witted and it reminded me of listening to my dad and his friends talking to each other at the Jamaica Club. I might not have been born in the Caribbean but I had grown up in a Caribbean household and this all felt very familiar to me.

And I felt welcomed at the club thanks in the main to one man. Guy Bailey.

Guy was at the heart of the club, a quality player in his own right, and a man who commanded huge respect. He took me under his wing and really looked out for me, guiding me during my time at the club. He would pick me up and take me to matches and bring me back. And as my career took off, he was always there supporting me and encouraging me. He was an obvious choice to join me at Gloucestershire as my vice-president and he remains a great friend.

Many moons ago Guy was involved in the Bristol Bus Boycott which exposed double standards on race grounds on the employment of drivers in 1963 and paved the way for the Race Relations Act of 1965. He is a true pioneer and someone who has done so much in his life to promote togetherness and understanding across communities, despite having been persecuted as a young man.

He is a hero of his time and I was lucky to be able to experience his kindness first-hand.

Playing for Bristol West Indies at that time was a good release for me away from a Gloucestershire set-up that was quite daunting. I would often be 12th man, running drinks in a dressing room that contained the likes of Mike Procter, Sadiq Mohammad and Zaheer Abbas. It could have been overwhelming but I kept my head down and got on with it and just tried to soak up as much as I could.

After that first summer around the senior squad I set about getting myself big and strong in the gym, and even though I had a three-year contract, it was only for the summer so during the off-season I had to work.

Most cricketers had to find work during the winter, and for some that was more fun than for others. Some players would go overseas and play in Australia or New Zealand, or even South Africa despite it being banned from the sporting world due to apartheid.

Some players would find themselves in the city or working in family businesses, but my dad was a welder and my mum was a nurse, so I had to find my own work. Over those first few winters I did all sorts of different jobs. I did some drystone walling, I worked for TNT loading and packing the vans, and I worked as a delivery driver for Matt Stevens Bakery.

One winter I spent in Manchester as a labourer, which wasn't a huge amount of fun apart from when my mate George would come up and visit me and we would go out clubbing and dancing the night away.

The good thing about the TNT job was that it was night-shift work, which meant that I could get into the gym and train during the day before grabbing a bit of sleep.

Once the cricket season was back up and running I could stop leading a nocturnal life and return to normal, although at that charity dinner Devon reminded me that we didn't always get to sleep when everyone else did.

Going out was something I was particularly good at, and I've met a lot of good people by enjoying my social life as much as I have.

In recent weeks and months my social life has ground to a halt, but as I have come to terms with my condition, I have been ready and prepared to see more friends than before. When small groups have to come to the house to say hello, I have thoroughly enjoyed listening to them talking and telling stories, even if it is difficult for me to join in like I used to.

Staying in is the new going out for me, and far from not wanting people to see me like this, I actually like the fact they want to come and see me and I can enjoy some time with the people I love.

My memories are still strong of so many fun nights and the sight of people having a good time. That is what I have tried to do throughout my life and whether it was with my training and my body, or my taste in fashion, I have always tried to look my best and put out the best version of myself.

That is why I think this disease is so particularly cruel for someone like me. If ever there was a disease that was designed to be the opposite of me, this is it.

I loved my muscles. I loved my clothes and my appearance. This disease has taken everything away from me. It has stripped me right back. My friends have all said to me, 'We don't care. We don't love your muscles, we love you, Syd. You're still the same guy that we have always known.'

But when I looked in the mirror and saw my body, I saw strength and confidence. Now that has all gone, and what am I left with?

Just the memories and feelings of a life well-lived, and that is what's sustaining me now as the end comes ever closer.

CHAPTER TWENTY-ONE

El Presidente

My voice has got so weak now that it is all but gone. I am having to use the automated voice bank that I programmed a few months ago when I was still strong enough to say words clearly and with a bit of volume.

The computer is operated by a screen in front of my face and it tracks my eyes so that the cursor moves as I look across the keyboard and I can spell out the words that I wish to say. Once I have my sentence completed then it speaks it out loud for me, in my voice. It is a very clever bit of kit.

I can also use it to send messages directly on WhatsApp which has given me back some independence when it comes to communicating with friends. That feeling of being in control of something as important as messaging has been a great experience to get back. It is such a simple thing that we all take for granted when we are fit and well, like walking down the street. But when it gets taken away from you without giving you any say in the matter then you really do appreciate just how wonderful that independence is. When it comes to the loss of my voice, of course I knew this would happen, but it has been quicker than I wanted and expected. This disease has got no class. It has no empathy. And it sure as hell has no time for doing me any favours at this stage. But what can I do?

My real concern now is my swallowing, which has become harder and harder as the muscles around my throat have become weaker. Even the act of taking on water is not a straightforward exercise.

Swallowing, like breathing, is a fundamental part of living. I used to be so meticulous in working out what food and drink went into my mouth and fuelled my body when I was training. If I couldn't swallow the right diet then I would never have achieved what I did in either the cricket or the bodybuilding world. It is another reminder of what I am losing bit by bit. This is another step towards the end for me.

This is where the disease leads. Losing my ability to walk seemed like the worst thing when it initially happened, but before I had confirmation of my diagnosis I was still able to look on the bright side of things.

I thought, 'If I'm confined to a wheelchair for the rest of my life but can use my upper body and arms, then I can take up something like wheelchair rugby'. That is a sport that I could really have got on board with. Maybe even the Paralympics could have been an aim at some point if I worked hard enough. But after the diagnosis, I realised that I wouldn't be able to keep the disease from attacking other parts of my body until nothing worked any more.

Watching the continued slide is so hard for those closest to you, and both my wife and son continue to be my rocks. They are my everything, but I wish I could just give Gaynor a big bear hug and tell her it will be ok. We still have that physical contact, but I can't be the one to offer it any more. I can't put my arms around her and show her how much I love her.

I am feeling hopeful that I still have enough time to be able to enjoy this summer because the cricket season has just started and it has brought the weather I love. The sun has been shining and the players have been able to start another season and bring joy to all of us cricket fans out there.

It is amazing what a bit of sunshine can do to improve your mood and outlook. I am trying to stay as strong as I can and it really is a case of taking each day as it comes. It can't be any more complicated than that for me right now and if I can make it through to a few events lined up this summer that will be fantastic. I know there is a game at Gloucestershire where they are going to be raising some much-needed funds for the MND Association.

Every bit helps and if I can add to the amazing work of people like rugby league legend Kevin Sinfield and his incredible fundraising in memory of Rob Burrow, then I will do just that.

I met Kevin briefly during his 'Run Home for Christmas' challenge when he came through Bristol and saw fellow MND sufferers and sportsmen Ed Slater and Marcus Stewart as well as myself. He is an inspirational guy and I am grateful for his efforts. Together we will help fund the research that will find a cure. The MND Association have quickly become a massive part of my life with the support and encouragement they have provided for me and my family since my diagnosis.

My care co-ordinator Keri Vickery has been simply brilliant in helping us to adapt to our new way of life and by pointing us in the right direction for all the resources we have needed. People like Keri make the worst possible period in your life that little bit better and it is appreciated so much. I don't know how we would have coped without her and the charity. That is why I'm happy to do my bit to help.

Whenever this brutal disease decides that it is time for me to go, I know that I will do so having lived a full and passionate life, and hopefully had a positive impact on the people I met, knew and loved. From a humble start in Gloucester I have travelled the world and connected with some incredible people with amazing talent. I am well aware that it is this game between bat and ball that will be the first thing that most people associate me with. And I'm okay with that.

Cricket has given me a lot to be thankful for, but our relationship hasn't always been smooth. In fact you could say that I have fallen back in love with cricket in recent years.

Having retired in the mid-1990s, I kept in touch with the game through a bit of media work and a handful of charity games. I played in memorial games for Neil Williams, another lovely and talented bowler who made it from St Vincent to play for England but was taken from us too soon at just 43 when he died from complications with pneumonia.

I hosted a couple of England supporters' tours to Australia in the mid 2000s which was a fun thing to do, but I didn't go any further with that and make it a regular activity.

My association with cricket was not as strong as it once was, but I maintained two important touch points with the game: my friendships with former teammates and coaching at my son's school. Beyond that, any involvement with cricket was by accident rather than by design as I focused on my business interests and bodybuilding career.

I certainly felt disconnected from the game.

Things started to change on that front when I was interviewed by a national newspaper about my bodybuilding and that seemed to strike a bit of a chord with people who were interested in my story, and I was asked to comment on a few cricket-related issues.

In particular I was often asked about the demise of Black and Caribbean heritage cricketers in the game, from a high point during my career when there was a healthy number of players who had emigrated with their parents in combination with a UK-born generation coming through in the 1970s and 80s.

But the flow of talent became a trickle.

I do think it is odd there have been so few Black players in the professional game in recent years, but it is down to a mixture of reasons, and not all of them bad.

There has been a dwindling of Caribbean cricket clubs across the country, so while Bristol West Indians are still going at their own ground, lots of other wandering teams have gone to the wall as a result of reduced participation and increased costs associated with the game.

Plus, we must remember that the options available to young Black talent in lots of sports and activities are through the roof and cricket is competing with them all.

One of the things I have been asked to talk about was my experience that day at Scarborough when the Yorkshire fans let me know how they felt about me and the colour of my skin as the club were starting to go through a closer examination of their behaviour towards Asian cricketers due to a complaint made by their former player Azeem Rafiq.

That long-running saga, combined with the death of George Floyd in the USA, brought things to a head in cricket and people started to look seriously at the way different groups had been treated in the game over the years.

I started to talk more about my experiences and I was even asked to conduct interviews and have conversations with Mark Alleyne and Guy Bailey for Black History Month to try and educate people about the need for greater respect and opportunity for all if the game is to be truly inclusive. Those interviews can be found on YouTube. I also took part in a documentary about England's Black international cricketers called 'You Guys are History' which was shown on Sky Sports across three episodes. In it I told my story about how I was treated by my own teammates at the start of my career at Gloucestershire, and as a result the club actually reached out to me to apologise for the way I had been singled out. That was a nice touch from their chief executive, Will Brown. He didn't have to do that but he felt it was important, and I took it in the spirit in which it was offered.

What I didn't expect was that it would lead to a conversation about how I could reconnect with the club after all these years and perhaps play a role in its future. We had a few meetings about getting involved and then out of the blue I was asked whether I might consider becoming club president. I thought they were joking.

It was an incredible honour to be asked and after thinking about what it might mean and talking to Gaynor about it, I accepted. I felt I could make a difference.

I knew what it meant to lead an organisation as I had been running my hospitality business for more than 20 years, and I knew how to encourage young people to make the most of themselves and how to build a collaborative environment. This role would be more ambassadorial than executive, but there was still work that I could do to really help push the club forward positively.

I knew that I wouldn't be a traditional president though, sipping gin and tonics in the committee room with VIP guests. I wanted to be a part of something meaningful amongst the community of the club. That means being an outward facing club to the rest of Bristol and beyond and making it clear that everyone is welcome to the County Ground, not just members and cricket fans.

I wanted to create more cricket fans from across the widest spectrum. That meant making President's Day a carnival atmosphere where Levi Roots could come and help with the food and local steel bands could play their music. I am a Gloucester boy through and through, but my Caribbean bonds are strong too and that is the case for so many people in our county who have heritage that stretches across the world.

They are all welcome, and that was my mantra.

Unfortunately my illness has rather stopped me in my tracks when it comes to continuing that role in a hands-on way, but hopefully in the short time I was able to influence things a message was sent loud and clear. I have every hope that the new chief executive, Neil Priscott, will keep the same approach going even when I am gone.

If the club ends up moving to a new venue to secure its future and provide a modern facility for a modern club, I hope it keeps hold of those principles, using it as a chance to open up and increase the love for it from a much wider fanbase – men and women, boys and girls from each and every community we serve.

My love for Gloucestershire Cricket Club is stronger than ever, and even through the ups and downs it has been a constant in my life. I'm proud to both have represented them as a player, but also now to serve as their president for however much longer I have left.

To be there at Edgbaston for the T20 Blast success was such a special day for the club and to be president when they won another trophy just filled my heart with such joy. It was one of the most emotional moments of my life and one that I wouldn't have missed for the world.

I am also deeply appreciative of my England career despite it ending the way it did and not being able to play the volume of games that I would have liked.

It wasn't to be for me, and I have made peace with that, but I am so happy to be a part of a group of people who have strained every sinew to try and win games of cricket for England.

What I never looked for or expected to receive was the incredible privilege of being named an inaugural recipient of the Honorary Life Vice-President Award from the England and Wales Cricket Board.

I received a letter from the ECB chair Richard Thompson informing me that the award was to recognise my cricket career, my involvement at Gloucestershire and the way that I have faced up to my challenge of living with MND.

It was another 'wow' moment as it showed me that just by being myself and staying true to who I am and what I believe in, I have managed to make a difference and positively influence those around me who feel I might be worthy of this kind of recognition.

I am still trying to lead by example in the way that I am preparing for the end and trying to do it with a positive outlook, but it isn't easy and I still wish I was dealing with anything but this.

These moments of recognition and the various events that are being put on in my name and that are supporting the causes close to me are making this time more bearable and are a huge support to me and my family.

It is that support from so many different people that has been truly humbling, from close friends to people I might have only met a few times but who have expressed the positive impact I have had on them.

In amongst it all there has been a friend who has been rather extraordinary in his willingness to be there for me when I need him. You will have seen the name George pop up every now and again in this book and for the past few months he has been by my side keeping my company, talking to me, playing me music and just helping to look after me.

I met George in the 1980s Bristol club scene when the number of venues for Black men to enjoy good music were pretty limited. It became a bit of a community because you would see the same people at those venues and George and I hit it off straight away.

We stayed in touch no matter where we were in the world and he began a successful engineering career with British Aerospace that took him to the Middle East, and to Australia which he loved after arranging a trip to visit me. He now lives there and is an Australian citizen.

We have been friends for more than 40 years so when he heard about my disease he planned a visit straight away to see both me and his elderly mum. He came to see me in hospital throughout his trip and promised he would be back when he could. He timed his next trip to coincide with that incredible charity dinner late last year, but he didn't just up and leave, he continued to spend time with me. When the date of his flight back to Australia arrived, we had a chat.

I was scared and he knew it. I didn't know how much time I had left. I still don't. But I know it is not long, I can feel the life and energy slipping away bit by bit. I didn't want to say goodbye to him. Not yet. I asked if he could stay a little bit longer. Neither of us wanted it to be the end, but it felt like it might be, and George made an incredible decision.

He said: 'Dave, I've got to go back to Australia, but I promise I will be back with you within two weeks. Let me make some arrangements.' He was as good as his word. He came back and has picked up his life in the UK for the time being, to be with me and help me. I cannot even begin to thank him enough for his time, his support and his love.

Between my wife, son, family and friends like Alistair and George, not to mention all those from Gloucestershire and cricket, the Trojan and bodybuilding community, Dojo and beyond, I am so blessed and grateful to have you all in my life.

Thank you.

Dave 'Syd' Lawrence
April 2025